ROUTLEDGE LIBRARY EDITIONS: ETHICS

Volume 13

MORAL THEORY

MORAL THEORY
An Introduction to Ethics

G. C. FIELD

Routledge
Taylor & Francis Group
LONDON AND NEW YORK

First published in 1921 by Methuen & Co Ltd
Second edition published in 1932 by Methuen & Co. Ltd

This edition first published in 2021
by Routledge
2 Park Square, Milton Park, Abingdon, Oxon OX14 4RN

and by Routledge
52 Vanderbilt Avenue, New York, NY 10017

Routledge is an imprint of the Taylor & Francis Group, an informa business

© 1921, 1932 G. C. Field

All rights reserved. No part of this book may be reprinted or reproduced or utilised in any form or by any electronic, mechanical, or other means, now known or hereafter invented, including photocopying and recording, or in any information storage or retrieval system, without permission in writing from the publishers.

Trademark notice: Product or corporate names may be trademarks or registered trademarks, and are used only for identification and explanation without intent to infringe.

British Library Cataloguing in Publication Data
A catalogue record for this book is available from the British Library

ISBN: 978-0-367-85624-3 (Set)
ISBN: 978-1-00-305260-9 (Set) (ebk)
ISBN: 978-0-367-46850-7 (Volume 13) (hbk)
ISBN: 978-1-00-303151-2 (Volume 13) (ebk)

Publisher's Note
The publisher has gone to great lengths to ensure the quality of this reprint but points out that some imperfections in the original copies may be apparent.

Disclaimer
The publisher has made every effort to trace copyright holders and would welcome correspondence from those they have been unable to trace.

MORAL THEORY

An Introduction to Ethics

by

G. C. FIELD
M.A., B.SC., LITT.D., F.B.A.

with a new Introduction by
STEPHAN KÖRNER

UNIVERSITY PAPERBACKS
METHUEN : LONDON

First published May 5th 1921
Second edition 1932
First published in this series 1966
Printed in Great Britain by
Fletcher and Son Ltd, Norwich

For copyright reasons this book may not be issued to the public on loan or otherwise except in its original soft cover. A casebound library edition is also available.

University Paperbacks are published by
METHUEN & CO LTD
11 New Fetter Lane, London, E.C.4

PREFACE

THIS book is intended to serve as an introduction to Ethics as opposed to a handbook or manual. The difference between the two, as I conceive it, lies in the fact that the one is intended to start the student on the subject and then leave him to pursue his own investigations, while the other aims at giving him some sort of assistance throughout their course. The manual, therefore, would have to give some account of all the chief ethical theories and all the chief ethical problems, whereas this is just what the introduction would avoid.

In attempting to write an introduction in this sense, I have followed a method, which is very common in teaching and lecturing, but has not been much used in published work. That is, I have taken, after a brief introduction to the subject, two specimen authors, or, rather, two specimen works, representing different points of view, and have examined and criticized them in some detail. These works should really be read by the student in conjunction with, or before, my own book. But to avoid overburdening him (or her) with too much reading at the outset of the subject, I have confined myself with slight exceptions, to the consideration of these two works, and have said as little as possible about the general philosophical views of the authors, or even about their other ethical writings. As I hope that this book may be of use to students who can read no language but English, I have quoted throughout from standard translations of the works in question. In the case of Aristotle's *Ethics*, I have used Peters' translation, and for Kant's *Fundamental Principles*, I have used the translation by Dr. T. K. Abbott. As this latter book is published in different editions in which the paging varies, I have referred throughout to the pages of the German text, which are printed in square brackets at the top of the pages in Abbott's translation.

After having suggested some possible criticisms of the theories worked out in these two books, I have then attempted to see whether it would not be possible to arrive at a satisfactory positive result by a modification and development of one of them. This occupies the latter part of the book. But all the conclusions in this part are only put forward very tentatively and provisionally. They are intended to stimulate thought and to suggest problems rather than to give a definite solution of them.

I owe a debt of gratitude to many friends who have helped me, directly or indirectly, in the preparation of this work. For direct help, I am indebted to my colleague, Prof. Alexander Mair, of this University, with whom I have been able to discuss many of the problems here treated; to Mr. W. D. Ross, Fellow of Oriel College, Oxford, who has been kind enough to give me his opinions on the chapters on Aristotle, which he read through in manuscript; and, above all to Prof. J. H. Muirhead of the University of Birmingham, who has read through the whole of the book in manuscript, and made many valuable comments and suggestions. Mr. J. E. Turner of this University has helped me greatly in the work of correcting the proofs and preparing an index.

Of all those who have helped me indirectly, I can say but little. But I must record a special debt of gratitude to my old tutor, Prof. J. A. Smith of Oxford, who first set me on the road to such understanding as I possess of Aristotle, and, through him, of Moral Philosophy in general; and to my pupils in four Universities, with whom I have discussed these and kindred subjects, and from whom, in teaching, I have learned more than I can possibly have taught them.

G. C. FIELD

LIVERPOOL,
    March, 1921

PREFACE TO THE SECOND EDITION

IN this edition I have corrected a few misprints and verbal errors. I have added one or two footnotes, and omitted a note on Beauty and the Æsthetic Experience at the end of Chapter XII, which appeared to raise more difficulties than it solved.

BRISTOL, G. C. FIELD
September 1931

CONTENTS

	PAGE
INTRODUCTION	ix

INTRODUCTORY

CHAP.
I.	WHAT IS MORAL PHILOSOPHY?	1

PART I
Kant: The Good in Itself

II.	KANT AND THE METAPHYSIC OF MORALS (I)	15
III.	KANT AND THE METAPHYSIC OF MORALS (II)	26
IV.	KANT AND THE METAPHYSIC OF MORALS: CRITICISM	37
V.	THE KANTIAN FALLACY IN OTHER FORMS	52

PART II
Aristotle and the Good as Purpose

VI.	ARISTOTLE AND THE ETHICS (I)	65
VII.	ARISTOTLE AND THE ETHICS (II)	79
VIII.	ARISTOTLE AND THE ETHICS (III)	91
IX.	ARISTOTLE AND THE ETHICS: CRITICISM	105

PART III
Towards a Constructive Theory

X.	THE CHARACTERISTICS OF DESIRE	117
XI.	THE DESIRE FOR THE GOOD	129
XII.	THE NATURE OF THE IDEAL	141
XIII.	REASON AND FEELING	155
XIV.	SOME MINOR PROBLEMS	168
XV.	ETHICS AND METAPHYSICS	181
XVI.	MORAL THEORY AND MORAL PRACTICE (I)	193
XVII.	MORAL THEORY AND MORAL PRACTICE (II)	204
	BIBLIOGRAPHY	213
	INDEX	215

INTRODUCTION TO THE 1965 EDITION

THERE are excellent reasons, pedagogical and philosophical, why G. C. Field's *Moral Theory* is still to be warmly recommended to anyone wishing to embark on a serious study of ethics. Its main pedagogical merit lies in its combining the advantages of a historical and a systematic introduction, while avoiding their respective dangers. A strictly historical introduction, by aiming at a complete record of problems and attempted solutions – trying to capture them all dead or alive – can all too easily blunt the student's awakening sense of proportion and lessen his power to discriminate between fruitful and sterile ideas. A strictly systematic introduction, on the other hand, tends to ignore not only abandoned *culs-de-sac*, but all approaches that are inconsistent with its own, and thus tends to obscure the important part played by the tension between rival methods and theses in advancing philosophical thinking from confusion towards clarity and perhaps even from error towards truth.

A combined historical and systematic introduction is very much preferable to either of these extremes, provided that the older ideas which it explains are still alive, and that examination of them naturally leads to the new ideas; and provided, of course, that such new ideas are themselves worthwhile. Aristotle and Kant, to whose moral theories something over one-half of Field's book is devoted, are important and influential forces in contemporary moral thinking as well as in contemporary moral philosophy, that is to say, thinking about moral thinking. In our actions and moral judgements we still tend to be guided both by moral principles and rules, to which Kant gave his main attention, and by moral ideals and purposes, which seemed central to Aristotle; and we frequently feel a conflict between acting in conformity with moral rules and acting in the pursuit of moral ideals.

This conflict, real or apparent, in moral thinking is matched by one in moral philosophy between so-called deontological (or rule-) theories, most of which can trace their ancestry back to Kant, and so-called teleological (or purpose-) theories, which go back at least as far as Aristotle. It would be easy to exhibit, for example, in the legal and political thinking of people as diverse as orthodox Roman Catholics and Fabian socialists, Aristotelian modes of thought; or to demonstrate the influence of Kant on the codification of the civil law of the Austrian empire.

Field could not have chosen his historical theories better if he had started the writing of his introduction today. As regards the systematic part of his book, it is more in harmony with the spirit of present moral philosophy than it was with the spirit of the thirties, when G. E. Moore's *Principia Ethica** and *Ethics* †came very near to being regarded as the ethical orthodoxy of the English-speaking philosophical world.

This does not mean that in the last forty years ethics has stood still. Without even an attempt to sketch the historical development, it seems fair to say at least that the arrival of logical empiricism in England and North America gave a new impetus to ethics in these countries – leading first to the so-called emotive theories, which deny all cognitive or theoretical meaning to moral judgements, and subsequently to subtler analyses of the function of moral terms and propositions. The situation reminds one of an earlier phase in the history of ethics, namely Hume's rejection of rationalist ethics and Kant's analysis of moral thinking as rooted in practical, as opposed to theoretical, reason.

However, recent emotivists, such as Ayer and Stevenson and their critics, differ substantially from Hume and his critics: Modern empiricism and emotivism is logical, in the sense that it is enriched by the results of over a hundred years of intensive and fruitful work in logic and the philosophy of language; and the same is true of modern anti-empiricism and anti-

* Cambridge, 1903.   † London, 1912.

emotivism. It is just possible that had Field written his book today, he might have added a chapter expounding the moral theory of Hume and examined some versions of its recent revival in the same manner in which he examines the revival, by some of his contemporaries, of Kantian doctrines. While it is quite unlikely that he would have been converted to their theories, he would probably have welcomed some features of them, such as their admission of the relevance of psychology and social anthropology to ethics.

It can also be assumed that he would have carefully examined some of the more important and widely read recent ethical works, which like their predecessors, consciously or unconsciously, start by rethinking and interpreting the theories of Aristotle and Kant. There is little in Field's book that needs 'bringing up to date'. This becomes particularly clear if one compares it with, e.g., W. K. Frankena's recent introduction,* which could with much profit be used to supplement Field's exposition.

Field conceives moral philosophy as the criticism of our moral categories, i.e., those fundamental moral concepts in terms of which the others are definable. Whether in this sense 'good' is the only moral category or 'right' is the only one, or whether 'good' *and* 'right' or perhaps some other moral concepts are to be so regarded, is itself an open question to be answered by moral philosophy. By 'criticism' he means more than analysis, either in the narrow sense of exhibiting the actual use of our concepts and the content of our beliefs or in the wider sense of further clarifying these beliefs by removing obscurities, confusions, and contradictions from them. Criticism in Field's sense, as in Kant's, has, besides that of analysis, the additional task of dealing with problems arising from analysis, especially the problem whether the beliefs analysed are, or can at least be reasonably assumed to be, true; and if so, the further problem of their systematic inter-connexion in the form of a theory.

* *Ethics*, Englewood Cliffs, N.J., 1963.

Some criticism, e.g., that of the medieval belief in witches, would have to stop with analysis. One would analyse such beliefs, find them confused and perhaps self-contradictory, replace them with something internally consistent, and judge them to be incompatible with the best available knowledge. This does not mean that there is not a great deal in nature, including human nature, which accounts for some people's belief in witches. But what accounts for a belief must be distinguished from what would make it true if it were true.

Some moral philosophers hold that moral beliefs are like the beliefs about witches not true of anything in nature or human nature, although, of course, human nature does give rise to them. But if by analysis we reach a consistent set of moral beliefs which is compatible with our best available knowledge and if the assumption of their truth is plausible, then the question arises how these beliefs can be fitted to each other and to the rest of our knowledge in the form of a theory capable of withstanding any objections of which we or others can think. A moral, like a scientific, theory will, if it is to give systematic unity to a set of beliefs, have to contain hypotheses which are not themselves among the unified set of beliefs. Such are the moral theories of Kant and Aristotle, and such is the moral theory which Field is trying to construct with their help. For, as he very clearly sees, the moral – like any other – theorist cannot afford to ignore the work of his predecessors.

Field's exposition of Kant's moral philosophy is clear and instructive. He explains Kant's so-called 'regressive' method, which consists: (i) in determining the concepts and propositions which are in fact employed in our thinking about what is and about what ought to be the case, and (ii) in distinguishing within these cognitive possessions, between that which is empirical (*a posteriori*) and that which is non-empirical (*a priori*). In applying the regressive method Kant nowhere considers even the possibility that the non-empirical concepts and propositions change or, more precisely, are being replaced by others in the course of time. Such changes have occurred in theoretical thought, especially in the physical sciences. In many physical theories Euclidean geometry and the principle of causality, which Kant considered to belong to the unchangeable core of theoretical thought, are no longer presupposed. In moral philosophy the rate of change, at least as regards the most general principles, seems to be much slower. Yet, as Field points out, even so a regressive analysis of Greek and of modern Western thought does exhibit substantial differences in regions of lesser generality.

Whether or not Kant was right in regarding the subject matter with which he begins his analyses as being the ordinary moral thought of all humanity is here of no importance, since Field questions not so much the appropriateness of their subject matter as their result, which he summarizes as follows: 'The essential moral fact is universality. And it is rational beings in virtue of their possession of reason, which are good in themselves, and therefore aware of and subject to the moral law.' The summary is, of course, no substitute for the three chapters summarized, just as these chapters are not meant as a substitute for Kant's whole theory of morals.

Field raises two main objections to it, of which one has often been made, while the other is Field's own, even though it may have been raised independently by others in a similar form. The first concerns the principal version of the categorical imperative which he renders as: 'I am never to act otherwise than so *that I would also will that my maxim* should become a universal law.' Like many others, he points out that we can think of innumerable examples of two maxims which are internally consistent, and mutally incompatible, and which can both be 'universalized' into internally consistent and mutually incompatible universal laws. For example, the maxim always to drink a glass of port after dinner and the maxim never to do so, or the maxim to get married at most once and the maxim to get married at least three times, can be so universalized.

Kant's mistake here would be so obvious and simple-minded that one feels tempted to interpret his words differently, even if this should imply doing violence to his literal meaning. One might especially stress the reference to willing in the categorical imperative and distinguish between: (i) being able to universalize a maxim without inconsistency, and (ii) being able to *will* the universalized maxim to become a law. Thus, I am able to universalize my maxim never to drink port after dinner (and even to accept it as a general guide for my own behaviour); but I am unable to will it to become a universal law. My inability to will this general proposition to become a universal law and my ability to will that no man be left to die of hunger are not a matter of logic, but of my nature and, possibly, of human nature.

Field's second objection is connected with his first. It is that Kant fails to explain how our knowledge that the maxim of an action would conform to the categorical imperative could ever move us to perform the action. For, while the knowledge that an action of a certain kind will have a *desired effect* can make us act, the mere knowledge that it is of a certain kind cannot. Again one might try to defend Kant by saying that the categorical imperative is not a principle of logic or classification, but a principle determining what it is possible to will. It must, however, be admitted that Kant's theory of the will is not clear enough to make Field's objections seem unjust. It suggests, however, further developments and anticipates some recent philosophical theories.

Kant distinguishes between theoretical reason, which apart from logic, contains the *a priori* principles which determine the general features possessed by anything that can have objective existence in a world apprehended by perceiving and thinking beings; and practical reason, which contains the *a priori* principle determining anything that is being capable of being willed by perceiving, thinking, and acting beings. Just as the principles of theoretical reason impose constraints on the merely logically possible, if it is to be objectively possible (if it is to be a public object for common sense and science), so the categorical imperative is assumed to impose constraints on the merely logically possible, if it is to be morally possible (if it is to be a practical maxim for action in a society of rational beings). Now Kant was no doubt much more successful in exhibiting the differences between the logically and the objectively possible than the differences between the logically and the morally possible. What Field calls the Kantian 'fallacy' seems to be rather Kant's failure to exhibit the latter difference than the mistaken assumption that moral principles can be derived from bare logical possibilities of universalization and classification.

If Field were writing today he might have considered some modern attempts at formulating the difference between logical and epistemic categories, on the one hand, and moral categories, on the other, as attempts at repairing Kant's moral theory in the spirit of Kant. The distinction between these two types of categories is, of course, at least as old as Hobbes's opposition between theoretical and practical absurdity. The interest of formal logicians in it goes back to the revival of interest in modal logic, the relevance of which to ethics was clearly recognized by G. H. von Wright, who developed his theories in papers and books since 1951 culminating in his *Norm and Action*.*

The revival of the Kantian approach to ethics and his distinction between theoretical and practical reason in modern 'linguistic' philosophy is obvious, once it is realized how easily Kant's notions of thinking and Reason can, in many contexts, be approximately translated by the linguistic philosophers' notions of speaking and Language. In a similar manner 'Practical Reason' can be translated by 'the language of morals'. The seeming need for supplementing the notions of logical absurdity, logical implication, and the rest by parallel notions of practical absurdity, practical implication, etc., in the service of ethics has – among linguistic philosophers – been emphasized mainly by P. H. Nowell Smith, who in his *Ethics* † tries to satisfy it by developing a theory of so-called 'contextual'

* London, 1963.   † Penguin Books, 1954.

implication', a relation which, however, is not yet analysed with sufficient clarity to serve as a reliable instrument of analysis.

Again J. L. Austin's distinction between declarative utterances, which are true or false, and performative utterances, which are, or are not, 'in order', reminds one forcibly of the Kantian distinction between theoretical and practical reason. Even when Austin in his later writings comes to doubt the exclusive and exhaustive character of his dichotomy and suggests that all declarative utterances might be performative,* it would not be altogether perverse to be reminded of the Kantian doctrine of the primacy of practical over thoretical Reason.

Field explicitly considers another attempt to save a substantial part of Kant's doctrine, namely Abbot's proposal to regard conformity to the categorical imperative not as a necessary and sufficient, but merely as a necessary condition of the morality of a maxim and the actions based on it. Since, however, Abbot seems to conceive the categorical imperative merely in terms of the logical possibility of universalizing a maxim, Field is right in rejecting this reconstruction. He would, however, have had more sympathy with R. M. Hare's theory,† which is in fact a reconstruction of the categorical imperative in terms of logical universalizability in conjunction with facts and inclinations and which claims for the so-constructed principle no more than that it is a necessary condition of morality. For Field objects most vigorously, and reasonably, to any moral theory which creates an unbridgeable gulf between what is good and what is desired.

Such a theory is the moral theory of G. E. Moore. Field's objections to it, though no longer a daring heterodoxy, and though nowadays almost generally accepted, are still important. He denies in particular Moore's thesis that goodness is a

* E.g. in 'Performative Utterances' in *Philosophical Essays* (Oxford, 1961).

† In *Freedom and Reason* (Oxford, 1963).

simple, undefinable characteristic. For if it were such a characteristic, 'being good' would not entail 'being desirable'. Moreover, since our mere apprehension of the good could not explain why it is – at least sometimes – desired, we could not explain the desire for the good at all. Field sees here a repetition of Kant's mistake, namely the assumption that the mere intellectual apprehension of a characteristic can move us to action. Moore's theory gives rise to this difficulty. Moreover, unlike Kant's – admittedly obscure – theory of the will, it does not give any hint towards a solution.

Field has much greater sympathy for Aristotle's than for Kant's position. He almost seems to think that Kant's importance lies in an important mistake which must be understood before one can profitably proceed in the right direction shown by Aristotle. He accepts the Aristotelian idea that all human activities are 'ultimately' directed towards one end alone, that it is possible to discover this end, and that its analysis provides the answers to the central questions of moral philosophy. He even shows great sympathy with Aristotle's famous principle of the mean which – unless supplemented by statements about the facts of physical and human nature – is as 'formalistic' as the categorical imperative, conceived as a merely logical possibility of universalizing maxims.

Field's interpretation of Aristotle is masterful. It goes beyond the literal meaning of the text to its whole cultural context with which he – one of the foremost classical scholars of his generation – was thoroughly familiar. Field's Aristotle is very much, what in fact he was, the pupil and disciple of Plato. According to Field, Aristotle's main contribution to ethics was his insight into the close connexion between moral goodness and desire – even though he did not fully succeed in elucidating it. He nowhere distinguishes clearly between the sense of 'desire', in which it is true to say that everybody desires the good, and the sense of 'desire', in which it is true to say that some people sometimes do not desire the good. This is Field's main objection to Aristotle's theory. Another objection concerns Aristotle's conception of the ultimate end of all human activities, namely the intellectual contemplation of the fundamental truths about the universe – a conception which does not seem to do justice to many of our simplest and apparently most obvious moral judgements.

It is one of the main aims of Field's own constructive theory to remove these two defects. At the time when it was proposed and opposed to the theories of Moore and Ross it may well have looked a little old-fashioned and perhaps even naïve to what then was the philosophical *avant-garde*. Today, as will be seen, it appears very much in line with the main stream of ethical thinking in the English-speaking world.

Field starts his exposition by analysing the notion of a desire. This analysis is not outmoded by any advance in modern psychology, if only because modern psychology is no longer interested in descriptive analyses. The modern philosophy of mind, on the other hand, has until fairly recently been less concerned with particular types of mental phenomena than with more general questions, such as whether mental phenomena are acts or dispositions, whether they are private or public, whether they can be analysed in terms of physical characteristics, and the like.

Having provided an analysis of desire, Field looks for a hypothesis with the help of which we could explain the difference between the two senses of 'desiring the good' which Aristotle fails to elucidate. A hypothesis which achieves this is the assumption that there exist objects which are 'so related to our natures that given complete knowledge and understanding of them, they would be desired by everyone'. If such objects exist, they would be desired by everybody who knows them sufficiently well, but might not be desired by those who lack this knowledge. But what kind of objects fulfils this condition? The answer is a further hypothesis, namely that of an ideal state of affairs. To have an ideal is to desire its realization; and we change our ideals as our knowledge of the world and of ourselves increases. However, what the hypothesis also implies is that in the light of full knowledge only one ideal would be accepted by human beings. The relation which Field assumes between knowledge, desire, and *the* ideal state of affairs is Platonic or could, without much violence to the texts, be read into Plato. But Plato's ideal city does not express Field's ideal, although he was very far from interpreting it as an unbearable oligarchy.

At this point it might be objected that philosophy should not propose hypotheses. But since rationalist philosophy – the impeccable deduction of conclusions from self-evident premisses – is impossible, since dogmatic philosophy is no longer (at least not consciously) pursued, and since there is no good reason why one should confine oneself to analysis, one can do no better than to propose hypotheses, provided that one is prepared to expose them to all possible objections. A moral philosophy, which is neither dogmatic nor narrowly analytical, must like science proceed by making and testing hypotheses, as best it can.

Field gives reasons why the moral ideal is a social ideal and why, in particular, it is best conceived as a community of conscious beings who love each other and act accordingly. This conception is supported by a descriptive analysis of the sentiment of love and its relation to knowledge and pleasure. He holds, again with Plato, that the moral ideal cannot be fully realized but merely approximated by human beings. Although not, except in a very wide sense of the term, a Christian, he draws attention to the person of Christ in which Christians see the most perfect embodiment of love.

Without going into details of the text of the later parts of Field's book, it is of some interest to point out that many contemporary philosophers arrive at very similar conclusions, even though they are on the whole less willing to admit that they are not merely proceeding by analysis, but also by proposing hypotheses. Frankena,[*] for example, holds that all moral duties presuppose the 'principle of benevolence' which

[*] Op. cit.

he defines as the duty to do good and to prevent harm, and which he identifies in part with the old dictum that 'love is what underlies and unifies the rules of morality'.

According to Frankena, and others, the principle of benevolence, though presupposed by all moral duties, and though implying some, does not imply all of them. If a necessary and sufficient basis of morality is to be formulated, the principle of benevolence has to be supplemented by the principle of justice according to which the same contribution should be made to the goodness of everybody's life and the same sacrifice be asked from everybody. Field, too, recognizes the principle of justice as a fundamental moral principle and regards it as expressed in Kant's second version of the categorical imperative, namely that each human being is, and should be treated as, an end in himself and never only as a means. Field, however, regards the principle of justice as a consequence of the moral ideal, which is richer in content than the principle of benevolence.

The difference between the two positions does not seem to be a matter of substance. It raises the interesting question – raised already by Aristotle – how far precision in moral thinking is possible and desirable. Moral discourse as part of ordinary discourse is not exact as are mathematics and theoretical physics, since unlike them, it does not idealize the situations which form its subject-matter. By artificially sharpening our moral concepts and propositions, and thus the logical relations between them, one may misdescribe their subject-matter and, metaphorically speaking, describe as black or white something that contains a bewildering variety of intermediate shades. A closer study of this question would lead one into a comparison between morality and law and into logic, and in any case does not lie within the scope of the book.

Field's constructive theory is not put forward as a final system, but as a provisional result of the co-operative activity of philosophy. Its content shows that the preliminary examination of Kant's and Aristotle's theories has been worthwhile, since it has drawn attention to fruitful questions and answers and since a great deal of these theories has in modified form been incorporated in Field's own theory. Thus, the moral ideal, though different from Aristotle's, bears the relation to desire which the Aristotelian theory suggests as a requirement for the adequacy of any coherent moral theory; and the principle of justice, whether or not it follows from the moral ideal, is a form of the categorical imperative.

In conformity with the British empiricist tradition Field does not regard the problem of the freedom of the will as directly relevant to moral philosophy. He regards it as one of those metaphysical questions, the answers to which leave, and should leave, any moral theory unchanged. He thus agrees with Locke that a distinction between free and unfree action should be drawn in such a manner that it is consistent with the strictest determinism. But if such determinism were true, moral praise and blame would have, it seems, to be given a different meaning from that which it ordinarily has. If the agent could in fact not have acted otherwise our praise for his action would have to be assimilated to the aesthetic praise which we accord to a person whom we judge to be beautiful, but whose beauty has nothing to do with his effective choices.

Field, however, rightly points out that any solution to the problem of freedom will depend on the answer to the question 'whether the category of causation as used in the physical sciences does or does not apply to human action'. That it does not is implied by the Kantian distinction between phenomena and noumena and, in particular, between man, as part of the phenomenal and of the noumenal world. Again, the existentialists, whose intellectual ancestry with respect to this question goes back to Brentano (even though they disagree with his determinism), deny the applicability of 'physical causation' and the other categories of the physical sciences to human existence. They oppose them to the 'existentials', which reveal themselves to a so-called phenomenological inquiry into self-consciousness. Field had little sympathy for the Kantian doctrine of noumena and even less for the existentialist account of human life, which he regarded as a mixture of a description of transient personal moods, and idle speculations.

There is, however, another – analytical – approach to the question whether and to what extent the category of causation (and, one may add, the non-causal categories of quantum-physics) apply to human actions and choices. Such an analysis was, for example, attempted by C. S. Peirce in *The Doctrine of Necessity Examined*.* It led him to the conclusion that all arguments in favour of mechanical causation merely 'prove that there is an element of causality in nature', and not that it is 'exact or universal', and that consequently nature leaves room for free action in a sense of a concept of freedom the applicability of which is consistent with the assumption of a merely limited operation of causal or probabilistic physical laws. A more radical analysis shows, I think, that all physical theories are, strictly speaking, not descriptions, but idealizations of experience, which can for certain purposes and within certain contexts – especially contexts from which interference by human action has been carefully excluded – be treated as if they were descriptions.

All this is quite in harmony with Field's remark that the question of freedom depends on the question as to whether the categories of the physical sciences apply to action. What he does not consider, however, is the possibility that the analysis of scientific theories may by itself show them to be compatible with limited freedom. And this point is worth some emphasis, since it is for the most part assumed, at least in the tradition of English and American philosophy, that only a great speculative effort can dispel the alleged *prima facie* evidence that the concept of freedom, except in the sense of Locke and his successors, is empty.

The progress of philosophy is not so rapid, even within its separate and, sometimes, separatist traditions, that any philosopher can without great loss ignore the classical works on

* *Collected Papers*, edited by C. Hartshorne and P. Weiss (Harvard U.P., 1931–35), Vol. 6.

his subject. It is also not so rapid that an introduction to moral philosophy, written by a man who combined the highest gifts of scholarship and pedagogical exposition with originality, should a mere forty years after its first appearance cease to be of very great value in helping the serious student to take his first steps in ethics.

INTRODUCTORY

CHAPTER I

WHAT IS MORAL PHILOSOPHY?

WHAT is Moral Philosophy or Ethics? The complete answer to this question comes more properly at the end than at the beginning of our study of the subject. But nevertheless we must make an attempt to give some sort of answer to begin with, if only to make clear to ourselves how and where we are to begin. It will be, at this stage, little more than an arbitrary statement of where we are to begin, of the sort of questions that we are going to ask and attempt to answer, and of the considerations that suggest these questions and their answers to us. And at the end we shall be able to make up our minds whether this way of treating the subject is a fruitful one, whether the field we have marked off for our investigations corresponds to a real line of division within the facts.

Moral Philosophy, as here conceived, is a criticism of our moral categories. Both the important words here need further explanation. About the use of the word " criticism," only a word of warning needs to be said. It does not mean in this connexion, as it too often does in our ordinary ways of speech, finding fault. It is used here in its original and proper sense of examining, of judging, of estimating the value of the things which are to be criticized. But the word " categories " needs further explanation than this. The word may be used in a strict, technical sense, as it is in Logic. But the meaning it bears here is a much wider and vaguer one than this, and refers to any of the big general ideas which we use in our thinking and talking about moral questions.

We all know more or less what a moral judgment is, and we are all, of course, constantly making them. So-and-so is a good (or a bad) man, such-and-such an action is right (or wrong), are two types of the commonest forms of them.[1] In such judgments, we use the ideas, or, to adopt our phraseology, the categories of good or bad, right or wrong. And in ordinary moral thinking we do not criticize these categories. Our interest then is centred in the question whether these or similar judgments are true or not. Is so-and-so a good man? Is this action right or wrong? We assume that there is something which we can call good or right, and we ask where it is present, what men or actions are good or right. But in Philosophy we shift our centre of interest. We are no longer concerned primarily with the question whether, for instance, any particular action is right or wrong, though we may have to raise a good many questions of that kind incidentally to our main purpose. The question that we raise as moral philosophers is, " What does good or right mean ? " What is the full and true nature of the facts which we indicate by these words ? Or—more fundamentally still—are there really any such facts ? That is, we are engaged in examining and criticizing our moral categories themselves, instead of, as in ordinary thinking, using and applying them in particular cases.

Such is the work of Moral Philosophy. And only a little reflection is needed to convince us that there is plenty of room for this work. We certainly have not got in our ordinary, everyday thinking a full and definite knowledge of what these categories mean. We do not form a clear and distinct idea of the full nature of the facts which the words used indicate. We can see that clearly enough if we look at some of the

[1] In ordinary conversation as a matter of fact, we are rather inclined to avoid the use of these terms for fear of laying ourselves open to a suspicion of priggishness. Most people would prefer to use some slang expression : " So-and-so is a decent fellow." " That's a rotten thing to do." But, of course, these are just as much moral judgments, and mean exactly the same thing.

actual ways in which the words are used. Take a word which we should think of as specifically moral, the word " ought," and examine the senses it bears in the following three sentences. "We ought always to tell the truth." " You ought to have taken the first turn to the right instead of the first turn to the left." " He ought to be clever considering what a clever father he has." In the first of these, we should say that the word has the specifically moral sense, whatever that may turn out to be. In the second it is used to describe the best means to an end which we desire, in this case the best way of getting to a particular place we want to go to. And in the third case it signifies what we may reasonably expect to be the case in certain circumstances. Our natural tendency would be to say that the word had an entirely different meaning in each of the three cases ; and we are all so familiar with all of these that it does not occur to us that there is anything strange about the matter. Yet there surely is a real problem here. If the things meant are really entirely different, how comes it that we use the same word ? Is it pure accident ? That would be hard to believe. And the only other explanation seems to be that we must have felt, without clearly realizing it, that there was some underlying identity in all the three cases, that there was something the same in all three that would justify us in using the one word. But what that identity, if there is one, can be, will certainly not become clear to us without much thinking : as we have seen, our first impulse would probably be to deny the identity altogether. Exactly the same problem arises if we consider the use of the word " good," another word considered to have a specifically moral application. " He is a good man." " He is a good cricketer." " This is a good knife." " This is good wine." Here again we find the word used, firstly, in the same specifically moral sense, whatever that may be; secondly, in a sense which implies that a certain person or thing is capable of doing a certain job or fulfilling a certain purpose, and thirdly, a sense which means simply that something gives us pleasure. Here again we clearly have to ask exactly the same question as before.

And this is not all. If we examine the ordinary moral judgments that we constantly hear made around us, we shall find that they are too often full of confusions and contradictions. We shall find that the moral terms are used and applied in a way which suggests sometimes that they mean one kind of thing and sometimes that they mean something else incompatible with the first. To take an instance. We often hear people saying of some action of anyone, that if he likes doing it, there is no merit in it for him. And then other people, or perhaps the same person in another mood, will say that the highest development of morality is to do right because we want to, to like doing right. The one way of speaking implies that the moral worth of an action is the sort of thing which is incompatible with any pleasure that is taken in acting thus, while the other involves the belief that the moral worth of an action, so far from being incompatible with enjoying the action, is positively increased by it. Or again, we often hear phrases used of which the effect is that a man must do what he thinks right, that he must act according to his conscience; that if he thinks a certain action is right, then that action *is* right for him, and he ought to do it. But if we put extreme cases to the man who talks like this, we shall often find that he will not accept the full application of his own beliefs. If we ask him, for instance: Suppose a man's conscience tells him to blow up a crowd of innocent people with a bomb in order to destroy a crowned head, or if it tells him to inflict the tortures of the Spanish Inquisition on those whose religious opinions differ from his own, can we say that in any sense he ought to act like that? We shall often find that the man who maintains the general proposition shrinks from the logical application of his own principles to actual cases, and that he feels obliged to admit that there are certain cases where it is wrong for a man to do what he thinks right.

We may find similar contradictions between our theory and our practice, between what we say we believe and the way in which we act. For instance, there is a very common idea that, in passing a moral judgment on a man's character, we must leave out all that is the result of external circumstances. We do not like to think that a man who has lived all his life in most unfavourable circumstances, who "has never had a chance," as we say, and shows the evil effect on his character, is really a worse man than one whose character has developed well in and because of a favourable environment. We imagine, more or less vaguely, a final summing-up in which all that is the result of external circumstances is left out. On such a view, external circumstances would have to be supposed to be morally of no importance. And yet the efforts that we make, in education, social reform, and the like, to secure a favourable external environment for people, seem to suggest that we do not really take seriously our professed belief in the unimportance for morality and for the moral value of individual characters of these external circumstances.

Other instances will probably occur to everyone. But those given are enough to show that the meaning we attach to terms like "good" or "right," the ideas we have of the sort of things that goodness and rightness are, so far from being clear and distinct, are ordinarily in the highest degree confused and contradictory. And this shows the room there is for the critical reflection on these ideas, which is the special work of Moral Philosophy.

It may, perhaps, at first sight, appear strange that we should be able to use such terms and apply them in our ordinary moral judgments without fully realizing what they mean. But the strangeness is only apparent. Of course, we must be able to attach some meaning to them. They cannot be, and clearly are not, mere meaningless collections of letters or sounds to us. But a bare minimum of understanding of their meaning is enough to enable us to use them in the way we do. We can do with an amount of explicit knowledge of the full natures of the facts indicated by them which is a mere fraction of what further reflection would reveal. And the reason for this seems to be found in the fact that, in general, we use them with a practical interest and a practical end in view. The practical effect of the rightness or wrongness of an action is that it has got to be done if it is right, and has got to be avoided if it is wrong. And for practical purposes that is all that we need to know. We could draw up a complete moral code for practical purposes, a complete list of right or wrong actions, like the great Catholic systems of Casuistry which have incurred such unjust obloquy, without knowing more about the meaning of right or wrong than this. Of course, as has been suggested above, in actual fact, our practical judgments of what actions are right or wrong are probably often affected by confusions and contradictions in our half-conscious assumptions about the sort of things that right or wrong are. And in these cases philosophical criticism will be of the greatest practical importance. But it does not seem necessary or inevitable that our unrealized assumptions should be thus inconsistent and contradictory. We might, theoretically, at any rate, so far as we have seen at present, purge our practical judgments of all contradictions, and produce a complete and consistent system. Yet even so, we shall have only come to the beginnings of knowledge of what good and right really are, and there will still be wide tracts of undiscovered territory for exploration by the moral philosopher.

This, then, is his work. And all the systems of Moral Philosophy really resolve themselves into an examination and a statement of what these moral categories mean. The next question to ask is, " How do we set about it ? " " What facts do we start from ? " " What are the methods by which we examine our ordinary moral ideas and assumptions ? " And—a further point of special importance to us—" What are the tests we must apply to any system of Ethics ? " " On what grounds may we reject some and accept others ? "

We must have some kind of idea of the answer to these questions before we can begin our special task of examining certain representative ethical views.

Moral Philosophy, like all other forms of knowledge, starts from and is based on certain facts which the moral philosopher has got to explain, and according as he is successful or not in doing this, so will his system be accepted or condemned. As has been said, his task is to give a complete account of the things which are meant by words like " good " or " right " or " ought." What we want to know now is, what data he has got from which to work, what the evidence is on which he can base the conclusions he arrives at.

The first and most important fact from which we start is the fact that we do make moral judgments at all. Yet even this apparently simple and obvious fact raises difficulties of its own. For we have to ask what a moral judgment is. It is very easy to say that it is a judgment in which we use one of the particular group of predicates, " good," " right," and the like, and assert it of any particular subject. But this does not tell us what we want to know. As we have seen already we sometimes use these predicates, the same words, that is to say, in senses which do not naturally strike us as specifically moral. On the other hand, as we shall see in some detail later, the characteristically moral predicates in some other languages do not really mean exactly the same as their nearest equivalents in English. The Greek word, Agathos, for instance, which we translate " good " would not convey quite the same meaning to a Greek as " good " would to an Englishman: the word would have slightly different associations and implications for him. And yet it is the chief moral category for him, and we call judgments in which it is used as the predicate moral judgments. What, then, is our justification for this? What is the element of identity of meaning which is present in both cases, to the Englishman when he calls anything good and to the Greek when he uses the word Agathos? What is the minimum which must be present in any idea to entitle it to be called moral?

We shall be helped in answering this difficult question if we recall the point already raised, that in ordinary use the moral predicates have primarily a practical bearing. And this reference to practice is one of the elements in the meaning of any term which must be present to entitle it to be called moral. In using the moral terms, good, right, Agathos, or whatever it is, we assume at least that they refer to something which is somehow a reason for pursuing those things in which it is present and avoiding those in which it is not present. We may mean something different in some respects by asserting that an action is right, and by saying in Greek that it is Agathos But at least we must mean this much in both cases, that this is some reason why the action should be done. But this is not all. There is always one obvious reason for doing any action, and that is that we want to do it. But that is not by itself a moral reason. We cannot and do not call a bare assertion of what we want to do a moral judgment. And so we get a further characterization of the fact indicated by a moral predicate. It is somehow different from our immediate desires, and may even at times be opposed to them. Further than this we cannot go at present. What its exact relation to them is, whether it is always and necessarily opposed to them, or whether it sometimes or generally leads us in the same direction, is a question which remains to be discussed. We have, then, got this further characterization of the moral fact, which it is our task to explain completely. We can now say that it is a fact that is somehow a reason for doing some things and not doing others, and that it is a reason for doing this which is other than an immediate desire to act in this way. Of course, we are only at the beginning of the search. But we have found some of the data from which to start. Any description of the moral fact which we can accept must at least describe it so as to show us how it can be a reason for action of some particular kind, and must distinguish it from our immediate desires. If it does not do this, the account will have to be rejected, because it has failed to explain the most fundamental facts from which we must start.

But this is not all the data we have. Besides the fact that we do make moral judgments, we must examine the moral judgments that we make, the particular things or kinds of things of which we assert goodness or rightness. This is a much more difficult task, particularly if we extend our researches beyond our own language and our own time. Besides this, we may examine what we may call the structure of actual moral arguments, the sort of reasons people give, when they do give reasons, for thinking that anything is right or wrong. And then, perhaps, we may gain some guidance from examining the way people act, the things they do, the motives that appeal to them, and the general psychological conditions of action. For instance, if a theory of what " right" meant described it in such a way that no one could really act in the way that was called right, we should clearly have to reject the account. The particular moral judgments of people we take as evidence of the sort of thing they imagine the moral fact (goodness or rightness or whatever we call it) to be. It must be, according to their idea of it, the sort of thing that could be a fact about the particular things of which they predicate it. Thus, to take a more general instance, we find in English that the word " right," in almost all cases where it is used, is asserted of some action or course of action. The word " ought " is used to express our relation to these actions : right actions are the actions we ought to do. " Good," on the other hand, is sometimes used of actions, but it is more often applied to individual persons : " he is a good man." But yet it, too, has a close connection with " right," because it would be universally admitted that the good man will do the actions which are right and which he ought to do. That is, the words are clearly used in a way which imply that they express different aspects of the same moral fact, and that this moral fact has a special relation to conscious beings and to actions. It must be such that it can be predicated of these; and it seems at any rate probable that it is not supposed to be predicable of anything else.

Besides these general features in our use of the moral predicates, there are all the particular judgments, all the things or kinds of things of which we assert these predicates. And it is in using these data that difficulties really arise. How much weight are we to allow any particular moral judgment as evidence? Obviously we cannot accept all moral judgments that are ever made as of equal value, because it is a familiar and obvious fact that they so often contradict each other from person to person, and still more from age to age. It is really perhaps impossible to lay down any definite rule by which we may decide exactly how much attention is to be given to each of the different moral judgments that are made. Probably each one of us will be influenced more than we should care to allow by the personal factor, by the greater or slighter resemblance the view in question bears to our own view. And this is not altogether undesirable. For, after all, the first part of our duty in philosophical reflection is to get our own views and all their implications clear. When we begin to try to do this we shall almost certainly modify and even reject a good many from which we started. And we shall work in the hope that a really complete understanding of all the implications of the views from which we started would ultimately bring each of us to the same result. In that faith we may suffer gladly all the misunderstandings and disputes which will be met with on the way.

Yet even if we could ideally arrive at the truth starting from our own particular moral judgments alone, the examination of the moral judgments of other people and other ages may in practice be of great help to us. And in dealing with these, we must at least have some idea of the way in which we are going to treat them. We shall lay it down, then, as a general principle that any widely-spread or strongly held

WHAT IS MORAL PHILOSOPHY? 11

view has at least a claim to consideration. We cannot be asked to assume the truth of all of them. But at least they may fairly demand that they should be explained. A theory which is to command assent must at least be able to show how such a view came to be held, what is the truth in it or the truth on which it is based, and how the error in it, if error there be, came to be made. One exception, however, will be made to this rule. If a particular moral judgment, a judgment that any particular action or kind of action is right or wrong, is clearly only a deduction from a general theory, which has been formed on other grounds, then the particular judgment has no claim to respect apart from the theory. It follows from the theory and stands or falls with it. It is then the theory that we must examine, not the particular judgment. Really, however, no particular rules of procedure which we can lay down beforehand can be more than the most general suggestions.

One more difficulty remains to be faced. We have spoken of discovering the meaning of the moral categories from an examination of ordinary moral judgments. But what does this process mean? What is it that we discover? This way of speaking suggests that everybody really means the same thing by the moral categories that are used, that the meaning that we shall finally attach to the moral predicates is in some sense what the people who used them meant by them all the time. But this raises a real problem. For we may well ask in what sense exactly the people who used these terms meant this by them all the time. It is very certain that, whatever our final account is, it will include very much more than people were clearly conscious of meaning in their ordinary use of these terms, and it is highly probable that we should find many people who at first sight at any rate would deny that they meant anything like this at all. There is only one assumption on which our way of talking and our mode of procedure could be justified. That is if we assumed that there was really something there, some real, moral fact, something different from our immediate desires which was yet a real reason for pursuing those things in which it was present and avoiding those from which it was absent. It is this fact that we have got to examine and describe as completely as possible. Almost everyone has seen that there is such a fact, has had glimpses of it, as we might say, on the strength of which in their ordinary moral judgments they have pronounced it to be present in some cases and absent in others, and have used it in a way which implied that it had certain definite characteristics. To continue the metaphor, these glimpses form our data from which we have to draw up a complete description of the fact in question. And we have to try to give an account which will reconcile and explain different people's statements of what it was they saw, trying to discriminate between what they have really seen and what they have, without realizing it, inferred from the glimpse they had. Just so, a skilled detective will construct a complete picture of a man who was seen near the scene of a crime at such-and-such a time by several eye-witnesses. They all agree perhaps, that he was tall, dressed in a light overcoat, and that it was not John Smith who passed often by there about that time. But one says that he had a beard, and another that it was only a scarf wrapped round the lower part of his face, one that he carried a revolver in his hand, another that it was only his pipe, and so on. Then different bits of further information will come from different people: one will notice that he wore glasses, another that he walked with very little noise, another will have noticed the road out of which he turned. From all these scraps of information our Sherlock Holmes will build up a complete description of the man, or perhaps identify him outright. He will have to allow for all the different factors which would influence the different witnesses, remembering that one is short-sighted, another imaginative, another only saw him in the dark part of the road. He will agree that under the circumstances it would be much more likely that the one man should mistake the scarf for a beard than that the other should mistake a beard for a scarf. And so bit by bit he will piece together the picture. And this is the sort of work that the moral philosopher has to do. But as the detective can only produce his picture on the assumption that there really was a man there, so the moral philosopher has got to assume to start with that there really is a moral fact to be described.

Now supposing that someone simply denies that there is any fact there, asserts that it is all a delusion, that there is nothing which can be a real reason for action except our particular desires, there is at this stage no conclusive answer that we can give him. Perhaps there is no absolutely conclusive answer to be given at any stage. But this is not a subject on which it is safe for us to dogmatize yet. At this stage we can only say that it is in the highest degree improbable that the practically universal testimony of all ages that there is something there can be entirely disregarded. The burden of proof rests on him. And we may venture to anticipate that he will not find it very easy to prove that there is nothing there, and to explain, as he would have to do, how so many people have come to think that there was. [1]

This consideration will perhaps give some idea of the task before the moral philosopher, and the conditions that he will have to fulfil. The aim of the present work is to examine some typical instances of attempts to work out a moral theory on these lines, and to see whether it is possible from an examination of these attempts to gain some guidance ourselves for a more positive treatment of the subject.

[1] Of course, it is just conceivable that the moral philosopher and the detective alike might eventually come to the conclusion that there was nothing there at all. But this would be highly improbable and would have to be proved beyond a shadow of a doubt. They could not start by supposing this even as a probability. And it would be absurd to suggest that it was incumbent on them to begin by proving that there was or had been something there before they proceeded to examine the available testimony.

PART I

KANT AND THE GOOD IN ITSELF

CHAPTER II

KANT AND THE METAPHYSIC OF MORALS (I)

THE first of these typical instances which we shall examine is the short work of Kant's, in which he gives a concise account of his theory of Ethics under the title of *Fundamental Principles of the Metaphysic of Morals*.

This work, as indeed most of Kant's writings, will probably appear to the student one of the most unattractive of the works which he is called upon to read. It is very rare to find anyone to whom Kant appeals at a first reading. The style is uncouth and the exposition extremely obscure. The conclusions he reaches seem particularly at variance with our ordinary ideas and our first impression is, that they are obviously absurd and perfectly easy to refute. The difficulty, indeed, seems to be to see how he ever got to them. But closer study will remove a great deal of this unfavourable impression. We shall see that he started from certain beliefs or assumptions about morality which we are all very apt to hold without seeing where they lead to, and that he got where he did simply by developing these. And we shall find that, so far from being obviously wrong, his general conclusions would be accepted by many modern thinkers, and that several modern theories of Ethics have a very great deal in common with his.

His preface gives us a fairly clear idea of what he was aiming at. We read, " The present treatise is, however, nothing more than the investigation and establishment of the supreme principle of morality " (p. 9). Or a little further back (p. 5), he asserts that it is " Of the utmost necessity to construct a pure moral philosophy, perfectly cleared of everything which is only empirical." That is to say, he wants to leave aside all consideration of particular moral judgments, all statements about what we ought or ought not to do in these or those circumstances. That would be a question of the special form that the moral law assumes in different particular cases. But what he asks is, " What is *the* moral law, the one absolute rule of conduct which is the same in all circumstances, from which the particular rules for the particular circumstances can be deduced ? " Or to put it in another way. When we say that different things are right and good, what is this rightness or goodness which is the same in all its different forms, and by what formula is it to be described ?

This, then, is what he is looking for. And his method of looking for it begins, at any rate, " by proceeding analytically from common knowledge to a determination of its ultimate principle " (p. 9). That is to say, he begins by taking our ordinary ideas about morality, analysing them, seeing what is involved in them, and where we get to if we think them out consistently. Indeed, he is pursuing this method throughout the greater part of the book. At the end of the second section, he says, " This section, like the first, was merely analytical." And in the same place he says that his conclusions have been arrived at " simply . . . by the development of the universally received notion of morality."

We shall find on examination that Kant started from, or was influenced by, several assumptions about what is good and right, which, at first sight at any rate, would seem thoroughly acceptable to our ordinary ideas.[1] What these

[1] He was also, no doubt, influenced (chiefly by way of repulsion) by

KANT'S METAPHYSIC OF MORALS (I)   17

assumptions are will appear more definitely in the course of his argument, but they may be provisionally stated as follows :—

(1) We assume that if there is a moral law at all, it must be absolute and universal. It cannot admit, for instance, of exceptions for particularly favoured persons. It cannot be suspended in special circumstances, nor can we alter it to suit ourselves or our own convenience. This is for Kant, perhaps, the most important of the ordinarily received ideas about morality. He says, himself, for instance, " everyone must admit that if a law is to have moral force, i.e., to be the basis of an obligation, it must carry with it absolute necessity."

(2) We assume, what is really much the same thing seen from a different point of view, that if a thing is really good, it must be good in and for itself. Its goodness must not depend on something else, and least of all upon its being a means to something else. For then obviously it is the something else which is good. This helps us to define what we are looking for.

(3) We assume that the rightness or goodness of an action cannot depend on what we want. Being right is quite different from being wanted or desired. We should even be inclined to ascribe an added virtue to doing right when we do not want to do it. And a further important point is that we want different things at different times, and that different people want different or even contradictory things. So that if the rightness of anything depended upon our wanting it, it would not be absolute and necessary.

(4) We assume that the goodness or rightness of an action does not depend upon its actual results. The results depend so largely on circumstances outside the action or the will of the person who acts, and so far as this is so the person cannot be held responsible for the result. And, a more important

certain philosophical views which were current at the time, and from which he strongly dissented, such as Hedonism, on the one hand, and on the other mere unreasoned dogmatism about what was right and what was wrong.

point still, if the goodness of the action depended upon the results, it would mean that it was the results which were really good in themselves, and not the action at all.

(5) We assume that the goodness of an action disappears so far as it is done under pressure from anything outside, so far as it is not dependent entirely upon the person himself. For then it would not be a free action, and the person could not be held really responsible for it.

Such, briefly and generally expressed, are the assumptions which Kant seems to have had in his mind at starting. It remains to be seen how he worked them out into a system.

He begins with a broad general statement that nothing is absolutely good in itself save a good will. All the other qualities are good only if they are under the direction of a good will : they derive their goodness from the good will and are not good in themselves. That is to say, to put it in more popular language, all that matters is that we should always want and try to do what we think right. It is not sufficient that we should merely wish to do right : " not, to be sure," says Kant, " a mere wish, but the summoning of all means in our power." Nor does it matter whether our particular actions succeed in their object. For that depends on circumstances outside ourselves, and we may be prevented, as he says, by " the special disfavour of fortune or the niggardly provision of a step-motherly nature." That, however, would not lessen our merit, which depends on our wishing and doing all we can to do right.

This general statement of Kant's is practically the same as the fourth of the ordinary assumptions set out above. Kant, indeed, really appeals to us to accept it on the grounds of its being such an assumption of our ordinary thinking. He speaks of the " thorough assent of even common reason to this idea." And the more or less popular appeals with which he tries to strengthen our readiness to accept it are not really intended to be convincing by themselves.

But these terms must be examined a little more closely,

if we are to get a clearer idea of what he means. In the first place, what does he mean by " will " ? We need not, at this stage, attempt an exhaustive definition : it will be sufficient to arrive at a general idea. Will is clearly very closely bound up with action. It is not the mere wish to do something, nor is it even the making up of our minds that we will do it later. The will works when we decide to act, not in the sense of the decision to do so at a later date, but in the sense of immediate effective decision. And this really amounts to saying that the will is the action. Why that seems perhaps a little difficult at first is that when we speak of an action we are rather apt to think of it from an external point of view, as certain visible bodily movements. But if we attend to our experience of our own actions we shall also recognize the mental side of this, the decision in our mind that sets our limbs in motion. The will is the action looked at from the point of view of what goes on in the mind. A good will, when active, is the doing of good actions. And Kant, as a matter of fact, uses the terms " good will " and " good action " almost indiscriminately.

So much for his meaning of " Will." But it is even more important to see more clearly what he means by " good," or rather, perhaps, where he considers the goodness to lie. A good will is the doing of, or that which makes us do good actions. But what makes the action good ? We have already seen that it cannot be its results or effects. It must lie rather in the motive, that which impels us to do or to will this action. But, if the action is to be good, this motive cannot be the desire which moves us to the action. We have seen already how impossible it would be to get any fixed moral law from the consideration of desires, since they vary from time to time and from person to person. But for the present argument it is more important to realize that a desire is always for something. And if we looked for the goodness in the desire we should really be forced to look further and to seek for it in the thing which is desired. That would really be to put the goodness, again, not in the action itself but in the effects beyond the action : not here in the effects which actually are produced, but in the effects which are hoped for or desired. And so, once more, we should not have an action good in itself, because it would derive its goodness from something outside itself.

Where, then, are we to look for that which gives moral worth to an action? Kant's statement of this is difficult, and must be examined closely (pp. 19-22). The action, he tells us, derives its moral worth from " the maxim by which it is determined."

The "maxim" is explained as "the subjective principle of volition." And he speaks again of the worth of actions lying "in the principle of the will." The principle of the will seems to mean, more generally, the reason for which the action is done, with the important proviso, in so far as the reason does not lie outside the action itself. But if it must lie within the action, it can only lie in the nature of the action itself. That is what Kant appears to mean in speaking of " what is connected with my will as a principle . . . in other words, *simply the law of itself.*" Here the word " law " is important. It appears, in this passage, to be used primarily in the sense in which we speak of a law of nature. A law of nature is really a statement of a universal fact about all the members of a class, a description of their general nature, or perhaps a universal connexion between some universal properties. Thus, for instance, the law of gravity is a statement of the fact that solid bodies attract one another with a certain definite force. This is a universal fact about solid bodies, it is a part of their nature. And laws of nature are thus more or less complete descriptions of the universal natures of certain kinds of things.

We may see reason later to believe that Kant himself was not always free from confusion in his conception of law, and not perfectly consistent in his use of the term. But we may be content for the present with the fact that this is the primary meaning which he attaches to it. So that the law of an action means primarily for him the nature of the action, its universal character. Thus he says (p. 20), that " Nothing remains which can determine the will except objectively the law " (that is, really, the fact that the action is of such a kind) " and subjectively pure respect for this practical law." The addition of " practical " is intended to distinguish it from other kinds of law. The law of gravity, for instance, that solid bodies attract each other, does not directly affect our wills. But the practical law which says that actions of this kind are good and therefore must be done is of direct importance for our wills and our actions.

But the most important new conception which meets us here is the idea of " respect." What does he mean by that? He admits that it may be considered vague. He defines it, in one place, as " the conception of a worth which thwarts my self-love." And a little further back, he says, " What I recognize immediately as a law for me I recognize with respect. This merely signifies the consciousness that my will is subordinate to a law," and so on. Or again, " The immediate determination of the will by the law, and the consciousness of this is called respect."

The upshot of this seems to be that it hardly ought to be called a feeling at all, though Kant speaks of it as such. It seems to be more truly the knowledge or the consciousness or the recognition of a certain fact. We respect the law simply by recognizing that it is the law, that the action is good and therefore must be done. What moves our will or makes us do the action is the knowledge or recognition—a cognitive process—that the action is of a certain kind, i.e., good.

Now if we have interpreted Kant fairly, there is the obvious appearance of a vicious circle here. The rightness or goodness of an action consists negatively in the fact that we are not moved to do it by anything outside the action itself. Positively, it is determined by the principle of volition, the reason for which we do it. The action is right, then, if it is done for a certain reason. But for what reason? We can only say that for the reason that it is right, and we recognize it as such. That is to say, it is right because it is done because it is right.

Now the circle as it presents itself to us did not so present itself to Kant, because he did not use the same terms. He used much more obscure and ambiguous terms which served to hide it from him. On the other hand, from a different point of view, Kant undoubtedly did face the real difficulty here presented in this form. Perhaps a little further consideration will serve to solve the apparent circle.

To do right we must act *because* it is right to act in that way. This is not a mere empty form of words. It at least serves to narrow down the field of action which we call right, by laying down that rightness can only belong to actions which are done in obedience to or out of respect for a law. We recognize these actions as being of a certain kind—good or right—in themselves, as being universally and necessarily such and therefore always to be done. And we must do them because we recognize them as always and universally and necessarily to be done, and not because of any particular appeal they make to us at that particular time or in those particular circumstances. That is to say, we must act by rule and with the rule in mind; each particular action to be right must appeal to us as an instance of a universal kind or universal rule of action. Or, in Kantian language, we must act thus in obedience to or out of respect for a law.

If, now, we want to put our difficulty into more Kantian language we should say, at this point, that the law according to which we must act seems to be nothing more than the law that we must act according to the law. And Kant would, in a sense, admit this to be true, though he would deny that there was any real contradiction or vicious circle. We find him asking (p. 22), " But what sort of law can that be?" Clearly we cannot look for it in any particular law which we can formulate in detail. Such a law would only apply to certain circumstances or certain special kinds of actions. Take, for instance, the commandment, "Thou shalt not bear false witness against thy neighbour." This law is absolutely valid, no doubt, and absolutely necessary. But it only applies in certain circumstances, when, that is, it is a question of giving evidence about another man at all. And there are numberless actions to which such a rule would have no application at all. It must derive its rightness therefore from some general fact which is present in it and in all other kinds of right action as well. And what we are looking for is a description of this fact. In other words, we want to know what is *the* rule or law of action.

Now, if we thus refuse to admit any particular rule, any rule that applies to particular actions or in particular circumstances only, as *the* moral law, what do we get left? We get, as Kant says (p. 22), "Nothing but the universal conformity of its actions to law in general." That is to say, we get nothing left in which we can look for *the* moral law, except the universal nature of law as such. And the essence of law as such is that it should be universal. We are left, as Kant would say, with the bare form of universality, which is the essential nature of law as such. And so we get (p. 22), the all-important first maxim, " I am never to act otherwise than so *that I could also will that my maxim should become a universal law.*" So that he does really accept the position that the moral law is simply that we should act in obedience to law, that is to say to law as such.

This is the essence of goodness, this is *the* moral law from which all particular rules of conduct are to be deduced. Kant proceeds to show how this is to be done, how particular moral rules follow from this. Thus we say that it is wrong to tell a lie. If we ask why, the answer is that if lying were right it would have to be a universal law. Everybody would have to lie whenever they spoke. But if we try to imagine a state of things in which such a rule was accepted, we can see at once that it would be an impossible one and that the rule would be shown to be self-contradictory. Suppose that such a state of things existed and every one lied, that is, said the contrary of what they believed to be the case. In that case, it would soon cease to be lying, because it would not convey a false impression and would deceive nobody. The possibility of deceiving anyone by a lie (and therefore the temptation to tell a lie) depends on there being some people or a majority of people who tell the truth. Universal lying is impossible or indeed unmeaning. Therefore, as we could not make lying a universal rule, it cannot be right. Or, again, we say that suicide is wrong. For if it was ever right, it would have to be right in itself, and therefore always right. That is to say, every one would have to commit suicide, so that very soon there would be no one left to go on practising the virtue of committing suicide. It cannot be universalized, and it contradicts itself if we try to universalize it. So we have here a clear test of what is right and what is wrong. If any sort of action is really right, right or good in itself, then it must always be so. If it really ought to be done as something good in itself, then it always ought to be done. And if it cannot be done always or by all people, if the attempt thus to universalize it as a rule of conduct breaks down and contradicts itself, then it cannot be right and good.

This, then, is the first stage of Kant's answer to the problem which he has raised. It is apt to seem to us difficult to grasp, perhaps even rather fantastic. As we go further into Kant's exposition of the subject, it will become clearer. But for the present it may help towards the understanding of it, if we consider it in this way :—

The question we set out to solve is, What is good? It is clearly a characteristic of some actions. We ask what characteristic it is, and the question is difficult to answer at first. But we shall, at any rate, be ready to admit that if any kind of action is good, in itself and not merely as a means, it must always be good. And if we ought to do the actions that are good—and to say this is really the same thing as to say that they are good—then it clearly follows that if one person at one time ought to do such an action, then every one at every time ought to do it; for, if good in itself, it must be good at every time for every one. And, conversely, if it cannot be made into a universal rule, if it is in the nature of things impossible for every one at every time to do it, then it cannot be good in itself. We should be ready, at any rate, to accept this as a practical test. But Kant goes further. He argues that if we think it out, we shall find that this fact —the possibility of being universalized—which we are ready to take as a test, is, in reality, not only a practical criterion but the very essence of goodness.

Goodness or rightness simply is universality, the being a universal rule, so that we have here, not only a final and complete practical test, but also, what we have been looking for all along, a statement of the essential nature of goodness. And with this he ends the first section of his argument.

CHAPTER III

KANT AND THE METAPHYSIC OF MORALS (II)

IN the second section of the book Kant begins the discussion over again from a different point of view. He now raises the question, what it is in us that recognizes or knows this law, or what kind of knowledge it is. And he is concerned to show that it is not empirical knowledge, but necessary knowledge, and therefore *a priori*. These are terms taken from Kant's theory of knowledge, a complicated and difficult subject which it is obviously impossible to treat of fully here. We must content ourselves with a brief summary, inevitably rough and incomplete, of the points in it which are of importance for his moral theory.

His theory of knowledge is based on the fundamental distinction between empirical and necessary knowledge. Empirical knowledge is knowledge of particular facts by means of what he calls experience, which practically amounts to sensation and perception. The essential feature of this kind of knowledge is that it gives us particular facts only and nothing universal or necessary. Thus, for instance, we perceive that this stone is falling to the ground. That is a fact of experience. But that by itself gives us no grounds whatever for asserting that other stones will do the same, still less for asserting that there is any law of nature that all stones or all solid bodies must act in that way in those circumstances. That is a universal, necessary fact. But we cannot have experience or empirical knowledge of such facts. Universal facts like this can only be got at *a priori* by the exercise of reason. And the exercise of our reason shows us, to put his view roughly, that they are involved in our experience, that they are the necessary conditions of our having experience at all. What our reason finds to be thus involved in our experience, we know as universal and necessary.

Now the moral law, if it is anything, is absolutely necessary and universal. Therefore it must be known, or recognized by the reason. We recognize it and respect it, and therefore act according to it in virtue of our being reasonable beings. Any other beings, therefore, which are endowed with reason must recognize it similarly. That is what Kant means by saying that it must be binding on all rational beings, and not on men alone, for it is not in virtue of our specifically human qualities nor under the particular conditions of human life that we recognize it, but by means of the universal reason, which, of course, we may share with higher orders of beings. Since, therefore, it is as rational beings that we are subject to the moral law, it is evident that the moral law must depend on and be intimately bound up with our rationality. And so, as Kant says, " since moral laws ought to hold good for every rational creature, we must derive them from the general conception of a rational being." Hence it becomes necessary to attempt some analysis and description of reason, or of a rational being.

With this, he begins an important passage (p. 36), " Everything in nature works according to laws." This shows, once more, how his idea of the meaning of law is primarily that of a law of nature. As we saw, the law according to which a thing acts is really only the statement of that thing's essential nature. He goes on, " Rational beings alone have the faculty of acting according to the conception of laws, that is, according to principles, i.e., have a will.' The essence of being a rational being is really twofold : (1) He is conscious of the law according to which he acts. That really amounts to saying that he knows his own essential nature as a rational being, or the essential nature of reason. (2) He acts according to the law of his nature as a rational being, not because this " nature " acts in or on him as some external force, but simply because of his conscious recognition of it as the law of his nature. The faculty of this kind of conscious action is what we mean by will. It may be pointed out, incidentally, here how this idea serves to make clearer the meaning of the first maxim. For the reason which finds the universal law of action really finds it in its own nature: the universal law of action for rational beings is really the essential nature of rational beings or of reason. And the essential thing about reason is that it is that which deals with universals and recognizes universal laws.

If, therefore, we human beings were pure reason, we should just act according to the moral law, that is according to our nature, of which we were conscious. There would be no sense of constraint and no difficulty, because there would be nothing in us which could possibly move us to act in any other way. This is what Kant means when he says (p. 37), " A perfectly good will would therefore be equally subject to objective laws (viz., laws of good), but could not be conceived as obliged thereby to act lawfully, because of itself from its subjective constitution it can only be determined by the conception of good." But we human beings are not pure reason, and that accounts for the fact that we feel the moral law, at times, as something imposed from without, something forced on us which constrains us and limits our freedom of action. Our will is not only determined by reason but also by other influences, our desires and inclinations. These are often opposed to the commands of reason, and consequently have to be controlled by it as something outside of and superior to themselves. That is why, as applied to composite beings like ourselves, we can speak of the moral law as an obligation, a command, or an imperative. It is the idea of the moral law as an imperative that Kant goes on to discuss. And he expresses what has been said by the words (p. 38), " Imperatives are only formulæ to express the relation of objective laws of all volition to the subjective imperfection of the will of this or that rational being, e.g., the human will."

He begins by laying down an easily understood distinction

between categorical and hypothetical imperatives. The latter are statements of the means to a particular end, for instance, you must do such-and-such a thing, *if* you want to produce such-and-such a result. They only apply under certain conditions. Into the general discussion of this kind of imperative and its further sub-divisions, it is not necessary to enter here. The conception is perfectly simple and intelligible. On the other hand, the categorical imperative must be absolute : it just states that something must be done, not from any reason except its own nature, any special conditions which make it necessary in order to achieve a particular purpose. It is here that the difficulty comes in : Kant himself says that " the difficulty of determining its possibility is a very profound one." But, at the same time, he holds that, if there is to be a moral law at all, it must be in the form of a categorical imperative. This, indeed, follows from all that has been said before. For otherwise it would not be universal, absolute, and necessary, would not state what is good in itself, always and under all circumstances, in a word, would not fulfil any of the conditions which have been laid down as the criterion of a real moral law.

For the present, however, we are not to discuss the possibility of such an imperative : one may leave it, as he says, " undecided whether what is called duty is not merely a vain notion." We are to confine ourselves to making up our minds, supposing there is such a law, of what kind it must be. " At least," he says, " we shall be able to show what we understand by it, and what this notion means." He then repeats an argument with which we are already familiar. The categorical imperative cannot command any particular sort of action. For any particular sort of action can only be done under certain conditions, so that the imperative would become hypothetical, and not of universal application. So we are left once more with just the universal form of law, the maxim that our actions must conform to law. And so we get again the first principle of morals, which is *the* categorical imperative. "Act only on that maxim whereby thou canst at the same time will that it should become a universal law." He then proceeds to apply this principle to particular duties, on the lines with which we are already familiar. And he ends up with an acute piece of psychological observation, when he says that when we do wrong—as in murder or theft, for instance—we do not ever, in fact, will that our action should become universal. On the contrary, we want other people to go on doing right, so that we can benefit by our wrong actions. Wrong-doing consists in making an exception for oneself.

We have now, Kant thinks, sufficiently shown what sort of thing the imperative of moral duty must be, if it exists at all. "We have not yet, however," he says (p. 52), "advanced so far as to prove *a priori* that there is actually such an imperative, that there is a practical law which commands absolutely of itself." He has found what such a law must be if it exists, and he now asks whether there are any actual beings to which it applies and in which it is realized. And to decide whether there are any actual beings which are under this law, he thinks it necessary to raise the question whether there are any beings which have a value in themselves and not as a means to anything else, in other words, are ends in themselves. Thus he says (p. 55), "Supposing, however, that there were something whose existence has in itself an absolute worth, something which, being an end in itself, could be a source of definite laws, then in this and this alone would lie the source of a possible categorical imperative, i.e., a practical law."

And he answers this question himself. "Man and generally any rational being exists as an end in himself." It is important, in this connexion, to remember that it is only in so far as he is a rational being that man is an end in himself. Kant repeats his old argument that, in so far as he consists in desires and inclinations, man cannot be so regarded. Desires are for something, and therefore they cannot be good in themselves. And the objects of desire depend for their value on being desired, and this they may or may not be, just as it happens. But, as human beings are ends in themselves, it must be in so far as they are rational.

But how do we know that human beings are ends in themselves, and not simply there as means to something else? Kant gives his reason (p. 57). " Man necessarily conceives his own existence as being so : so far then this is a subjective principle of human actions. But every other rational being regards its existence similarly, just on the same rational principle that holds for me : so that it is at the same time an objective principle." That is to say, each one of us recognizes that he is an end in himself, and that he does not need his existence to be justified as a means to something else. And further reflection will show us, as seen above, that it is as a rational being that each of us is an end in himself. If, therefore, it is being a rational being that makes each man an end in himself, it follows that the same thing must apply to all rational beings. It is part of their nature as rational beings. So our reason recognizes all rational beings as ends in themselves, and therefore bids us to treat them as such, even if our inclinations sometimes urge us to regard ourselves as an end and all other human beings as means. That would be essentially self-contradictory and reason forbids it. And so we get the further law : " So act as to treat humanity, whether in thine own person or that of any other, in every case as an end withal, never as means only "

Leaving aside, now, the practical applications of this which come after the formulation of the law, we must turn our attention to certain more general deductions which follow from it. We have now got a universal law of action which is based on the nature of rational beings. The law, in fact, is really a statement of the essential facts about rational beings : the law which they recognize is their own nature. Hence we must not think of rational beings merely as being subject to law. The law arises from their own nature, so that in a real sense they must be thought of also as lawgivers. So we get what Kant calls the third practical principle of the will, that is (p. 60), " the idea of the will of every rational being as a universally legislative will." " Thus," he says, " the will is not simply subject to the law, but so subject that it must be regarded as itself giving the law, and on this ground only, subject to the law (of which it can regard itself as the author)." The practical reason—the reason that deals with action, which is the same thing as the will of a rational being— is, then, the law-giver. For the law depends on its nature. But as its nature as reason is to deal with universals and to be universal in its application, it follows that its laws must be universal, that is, its rules of action must be universally applicable. So if each rational being gives laws that are universally applicable, then the law or principles of action of each rational being must not clash with those of any other, but must work in together with them. And thus we reach the conception of a kingdom of ends, " all ends combined in a systematic whole." Each human being, or each rational being is a member of this kingdom of ends both as legislator and as subject. Of course, as we are none of us purely rational, it is, as Kant says, only an ideal, and in practice the ends which different human beings actually do pursue only too often clash.

We now get to a complete account of the moral law, and Kant explains in his own terms its full nature and the relation of the three formulæ already given to one another. We have first the form, or the general description of it. The essential point in this is that it must be universal in its application. Then we have the matter, or the particular things to which the general law applies or in which it is found. These are rational beings, human beings in so far as they are rational and any other rational beings that there may be. As they are rational, that is, conscious of the law, we may speak of them as obeying it, an expression which could not strictly be used of the relation of unconscious, material things to the law of their being. Finally we get " the totality of the system of these," that is, of the different particular things united together in a system by their obedience to the general law of this common nature. And so, we get the kingdom of ends.

This concludes the second section of the book, and with it the most important part of the argument for our purposes. But Kant is not content to leave the matter here. He says that we have shown that morality is essentially bound up with the autonomy of the will, with reason as self-legislative. But we have not yet shown that " morality is no creation of the brain." We have not shown that it is possible, that reason can be self-legislative and capable of laying down moral laws. He proceeds to attempt this task in the third section, and in the course of his argument throws some fresh light on the important points already raised. Otherwise the examination of the section need not detain us long. It raises some points of great interest for the consideration of his general philosophical position, but its specifically ethical importance is small.

The first point which needs some explanation is the passage at the beginning of the section, where he talks about the difference between autonomy and heteronomy, between rational freedom and physical necessity. By freedom, he explains, he does not mean just caprice, the entire absence of any law by which to act. The will, or the practical reason, is free if and in so far as it acts purely from its own law, the law of its own nature. Of course, in a sense, physical things act according to the law of their own nature: the stone, for instance, falls to the earth because it is part of its own nature as a solid body to do so. But the important difference, which forbids us to assert freedom in this case, is that the physical thing can only act according to the law of its nature if it is set going, as it were, by some thing or some force outside it. There has to be an external stimulus.

Nothing in physical nature could act quite by itself. A tree falls. It does so partly because it is its nature as a solid body to gravitate to the earth. But that is not the whole cause of the event. There must be something, as we say, to make it fall: perhaps the soil round its roots has been loosened by rain, or it has been struck by lightning. So it is all through nature, which is what Kant is referring to in speaking about the efficient cause according to which everything acts. That is why these things are not free or autonomous, because the way they act is partly, at any rate, controlled by events outside themselves.

Thus to be autonomous or free a thing would have to act simply from its own nature, without being in any way controlled or stimulated by any efficient cause outside itself. If the will is free, it would have to act in this way. And what he is now concerned to prove is the possibility of anything which can act in this way. He wants, that is, to prove the existence of a " pure self," a self which can act without any stimulus from outside[1] in the way described. As he attaches so much importance to the proof, it is necessary to say something about it, though it really concerns his general philosophical position rather than his ethical views.

This " proof " of the existence of a pure self is on lines analogous to his well-known proof of the existence of things in themselves. What that proof is can only be very briefly and inadequately touched on here. Experience, he says, only tells us of things as they affect us. Or, to put it in a less controversial way, experience only gives us the appearance of things, how they look or appear to us. Or, at least, it only gives us the sensible qualities of things, their colour, etc. But if we reflect on it, reason shows us that there must be a thing *which* looks like that, which has these qualities,

---

[1] Or rather uncontrolled by any stimulus from outside. Even Kant would admit that the exercise of human freedom is in reply to the stimulus of an occasion. But the character of the action, which makes it right, is not determined by the special characteristics of the external circumstances.

or which affects us in that way. We cannot say anything about it, because anything we could say would be giving its qualities, not it. But it is a necessary assumption that it is there. Now, to apply this to the self. The self, as we experience it, is in the midst of an external world, and is constantly being affected by the things around it and reacting to them by the emotions which they arouse in it. That is the empirical self. But the very fact of our experience of this involves the existence of what we might call a self in itself, behind all these things, the something which is acted on by them and reacts in different ways. Or in other words, the will controlled, as we see it, by all these external influences implies a will in itself, a pure will behind all this. And if we consider this, we find we have got the pure self that we want. This is a very rough and incomplete summary of Kant's view. And with this we conclude the last section of the book.

It is not easy to sum up the results of this exposition in a few sentences. Kant starts by looking for a rule of conduct or moral law which shall be absolutely necessary and universal. And he finds that you cannot lay down any particular rule of conduct as being the universal rule. Not that, if it is a true rule, there will be any exceptions to it, but because no particular rule will apply universally, there will be other rules wanted for other relations of life. So we find that the only thing left that we can say about the moral law is that it must be universal. That fact which we admitted to be the test of it, we now find to be the essential thing about it. And all particular rules must be deduced from this, by seeing whether they can be universalized or not. They cannot, of course, be universalized in one sense, because they cannot cover all the relations of life or apply to all kinds of action. But when we speak of some particular rule—"Thou shalt not steal," for instance—being made a universal rule, we really are using universal in a slightly different sense to mean a rule which admits of no exceptions in the circumstances in which it could be applied at all. There are no cases where it could apply to which it does not. The opposite rule could never hold good. There is no real difficulty in this distinction.

This, then, is the moral law. Anything which acts according to that law will be good in itself, and conversely anything good in itself must act according to that law. But are there any such beings? He does not ask whether there are, in fact, any beings which do actually act according to that law. That would involve empirical investigations of an insuperable difficulty. He begins rather at the other end, and asks if there are any beings which we must conceive of as being good in themselves or ends in themselves. There must be such beings, he considers: because we cannot think of everything only as having value as a means to something else. That would land us in an infinite regress. So we find such beings in man, in so far as he is rational, and in general in any rational being. We have already seen the arguments by which this is proved, and the consequences he draws from it. But these are the two important points of the theory which must be grasped. The essential moral fact is universality. And it is rational beings, in virtue of their possession of reason, which are good in themselves, and therefore aware of and subject to the moral law. All the rest of the discussion centres round these two points. With this we must conclude the exposition of Kant's moral theory.

CHAPTER IV

KANT AND THE METAPHYSIC OF MORALS: CRITICISM

IN criticisms of Kant's ethical theory in text-books of Philosophy and elsewhere, we often find the chief emphasis laid on the supposed practical consequences of Kant's view, which are represented as being obviously at variance with our ordinary moral ideas, and in some cases amounting almost to a *reductio ad absurdum* of his whole theory.

It is argued, for instance, that none of these so-called moral rules can really be universalized in practice. The rule, Thou shalt not lie, for instance, leads to the conclusion that if a man pursued by murderers could be saved by a timely lie, it would nevertheless be wrong for us to tell this lie, and that it would be our duty to help the murderers to commit the crime by telling them which way their victim had gone. Kant, indeed, seems ready to accept this conclusion. But almost every one would feel that a conclusion like this violates our strongest moral feelings, and that a view which really led to this conclusion would have to be abandoned. Or again, "Thou shalt not kill," if universalized, would forbid war, capital punishment, and even legitimate self-defence or defence of other people. And, though there are people who have gone to these lengths, it is certain that the moral sense of the majority of mankind is against them. We should say that "Thou shalt not kill," is a sound rule, in general, but that there are circumstances in which we may or must break it. If we modify the rule and say, "Thou shalt not kill, except under certain circumstances," to make it a universal and at the same time a practical rule we should have to mention all the circumstances in the formula. And if we try we shall find this absolutely impossible. Thus if we say that one may kill in defence of the life of another, we find that this would not apply if the other was a murderer we were defending from justice. If we say that one may kill in defence of the life of another who ought not to be killed, then of course we have said nothing. We have only raised the question again when or under what circumstances ought or ought not a man to be killed, which is just the question we are asking.

We can strengthen this line of argument by finding cases of actions which would be universally recognized as good and yet which could not possibly be universalized, where the attempt to universalize them would lead to as great logical absurdities as universal lying. Take the question of self-sacrifice, for instance. The universal moral sentiment of mankind recognizes self-sacrifice as a great good. Yet the attempt to universalize it would be absolutely self-contradictory. For self-sacrifice, giving up what we want ourselves to other people, involves for it to be possible the existence of other people who accept the sacrifice. But if every-one is sacrificing himself, there will be no one to accept the sacrifice, and self-sacrifice itself becomes impossible.

The same question, really, comes up from a different point of view when we find two principles of action, both apparently right, clashing with each other. We have the rule forbidding the telling of lies. And we have another rule bidding us preserve innocent human life by every means in our power. Both these would be recognized as wholly laudable principles of action. But, as we have seen, in the case of the man escaping from murderers they come into conflict. If we ask how we are to decide between them, all we can say is that it depends on the circumstances of the particular case. But with that we have already abandoned Kant's principle. We recognize that it is impossible to have any general rule, absolutely universal and admitting of no exceptions. We cannot lay down beforehand a general formula which can be applied ready-made to each particular case. We have to examine each particular case on its merits, because we never can be sure beforehand that its special circumstances will not be of importance.

We shall probably be ready to accept all that is said in criticism of this kind as quite true. And, if it is true, as against Kant's exposition of his system it is perfectly conclusive, so far as it goes. There can be no doubt that he really thought that he had got hold of a principle of supreme importance for practice, which would really enable us to decide in actual cases what we ought or ought not to do. And equally without doubt is it, if there is anything in the above criticisms, that he had not in fact found such a principle. We cannot apply his test, as he thought we could, to all practical cases. But, in spite of all this, it still remains open to question whether these objections are fatal to the Kantian system as a whole. They are fatal to the practical conclusions that Kant draws from the central and fundamental points of his system. But it remains to be seen whether it was really necessary to draw these conclusions. It is still possible that we may be able to abandon these conclusions, against which we have found such decisive objections, and yet still retain these central and fundamental points.

If we wished to essay this kind of salvage work, we should probably argue something in these terms:—Let us admit, we should say, that we cannot get a definition or account of the good which we can use as an absolute criterion to decide in each particular case what is right or not. But that is not to admit that Kant's general account of what constitutes good or right is false: it merely shows that we cannot use his definition in the way he thought that we could. Still less is it to say that no general account of the nature of goodness or rightness is possible. But it does say that any general account of the good that we get will have to be *ex post facto*. That is to say, after we have decided that a particular action or kind of action is good or right, we can look for and discover in it what it was that made it good or right.

This procedure may be illustrated from other subjects of philosophical investigation. Thus the general account of the nature of causation, which Philosophy tries to arrive at, would not help us to decide in any particular case what was the cause of what. It would only enable us to say what the general nature of the connexion was, which we had already discovered to exist between certain things. Or again, we might arrive at a definition of truth, we might come to the conclusion that it was the agreement of two ideas or the agreement of an idea with reality or any other of the definitions which different schools of philosophers have mentioned. But whatever definition we adopt, it will be derived from an examination of instances of propositions which are true. And it will not enable us to tell whether any proposition is true or false. At the most, it tells us the exact meaning of the question we are asking when we ask whether any particular proposition is true or false.

Now this distinction was perfectly familiar to Kant, who was probably, indeed, the first person who really grasped it. But he does not seem to have applied it, as we might have expected him to do, to his moral theory. But if we apply it, as he ought to have done, we shall no longer ask or expect that our account of the nature of good should give us a practical criterion which would decide at once whether any particular action was right or wrong. The most we can expect of it is that it should help us to get clear in our own minds about the real nature of the question we ought to ask in particular moral cases.

This it does do when it tells us that the essence of the rightness of an action is its universality. But here we come up against the objection already given that this is impossible, because there is really no such thing as universality in moral precepts. As we saw, all so-called rules of right conduct have exceptions in certain cases, and each case has to be considered on its merits. For the possibility of a universal rule applying to more actions than one, depends upon these different actions being of the same kind. And, of course, as a matter of fact no action is exactly the same as any other in all its circumstances, and we can never say beforehand that its special circumstances are irrelevant to its moral worth. So that really we should need a special rule for each action.

"Well," the reply to this objection would be, "and why not?" For, it would be urged, this argument really rests on a confusion about the meaning of universality. It would apply equally, for instance, against the Law of the Uniformity of Nature. We express this law by saying that the same causes always produce the same effects. But of course we know all the time really that there never is exactly the same cause or the same effect repeated: exactly the same event or series of events never does and never can occur twice over. But that does not invalidate the law, if we understand it rightly. For universality does not necessarily involve there being actually more than one case of a particular law. Perhaps there would be less danger of confusion if, for the misleading word " universality," we substituted a word such as " necessity," which is really a better expression of the same idea. We should then say that the Law of the Uniformity of Nature means that the cause is necessarily connected with the effect. And in a moral question we should say that this action is necessarily right, that it necessarily follows from all these circumstances that the action should be done. We may say, if we like, that if *per impossibile* we could get exactly the same circumstances over again, exactly the same action would have to be done. The fact that exactly the same circumstances cannot really be repeated does not make this an empty phrase. We can surely attach some meaning to the question, Supposing that anyone else were in exactly the same circumstances, should we will him to act in this way? even though, as a matter of fact, no one else is or ever could be in exactly the same circumstances. In fact, this is really the right question to ask, the right attitude in which to approach particular moral problems. And so universality or necessity can be maintained to be the essence of rightness or goodness, even though it does not give us the infallible practical guidance that Kant expected from it.

Besides this we have a contribution of more practical value in the second maxim which bids us always treat humanity, whether in oneself or in others, as an end not as a means. The wrongness of treating any human being as a means is deduced, of course, from the first maxim. It is wrong, because we do not will that anyone else should treat all other people, including ourselves, merely as a means. But this rule is really of more practical value than the first maxim and in some cases can be applied as a practical test. Not that it is always a sufficient guide by itself, because there might be cases where there was an honest difference of opinion whether a particular course of action did involve treating any human beings merely as a means or not. And we may allow, in general, that Kant does not help much to resolve honest doubts and difference of opinion. But he shows us the right questions to ask, and he prevents us, if we follow him, from allowing our own wishes to blind us to what is right.

We may sum up, then, by saying that although we cannot apply his tests in practice with the certainty that he claimed for them, yet there is no reason why we should not accept them as really a correct account of what right action consists in.

So far the case for the defence. And as against the criticisms previously advanced, it seems sound enough. It preserves the essence of the doctrine, while recognizing that we must drop certain applications of it which were originally made. But we must not think that with this the whole case against Kant's ethical theory falls to the ground. There are far more serious and fundamental objections to his view, which we must now consider.

We shall find that the previous objection, even though we do not think it holds good by itself, will suggest to us the lines on which a much more serious attack may be launched.

For it is, after all, by a consideration of its practical consequences that we begin to find the view unsatisfactory.

Probably we should all feel that no one would be really satisfied by being told that good or right merely meant necessary or capable of universal application or any other term of this kind. Of course, a vague feeling like that would not by itself be decisive against the view, though it might raise a doubt whether the view was really derived so directly from our universally received notions of morality as was claimed. But, apart from what has been already discussed, we shall find on further consideration some practical consequences of the view which will certainly give us pause before accepting it. We must remember that, according to Kant, this is the essential nature of the good, and not merely one of its qualities. It is what goodness means. And, if that is so, we may invert the proposition, All good or right actions can be universalized, into, Anything that can be universalized is good or right. And the consequences of that are much more serious than those mentioned in the previous objections. In fact, they are such as we could hardly accept. Truth-telling, for instance, certainly can be universalized as a practical law. And yet we have seen extreme cases where, according to our ordinary moral ideas, it is not right to tell the truth.

The point will become even clearer if we consider the very significant passage in which Kant discusses the practical application of his own maxims (pp. 49, 50). " A third finds in himself a talent which with the help of some culture might make him a useful man in many respects. But he finds himself in comfortable circumstances, and prefers to indulge in pleasure rather than to take pains in enlarging and improving his happy natural capacities. He asks, however, whether his maxim of neglect of his natural gifts, besides agreeing with his inclination to indulgence, agrees also with what is called duty. He sees then that a system of nature could indeed subsist with such a universal law although men (like the South Sea islanders) should let their talents rust, and resolve to devote their lives merely to idleness, amusement, and propagation of their species—in a word to enjoyment; but he cannot possibly *will* that this should be a universal law of nature, or be implanted in us as such by a natural instinct. For, as a rational being, he necessarily wills that his faculties be developed, since they serve him, and have been given him, for all sorts of possible purposes."

Even more striking, perhaps, is his next imaginary case, of the man who declares that he will not help others who are in misfortune, even when it is in his power. Of course, as Kant sees, it would be a quite possible universal law that none should help others in misfortune. "But," he asserts, " although it is possible that a universal law of nature might exist in accordance with that maxim, it is impossible to *will* that such a principle should have the universal validity of a law of nature. For a will which resolved this would contradict itself, inasmuch as many cases might occur in which one would have need of the love and sympathy of others, and in which, by such a law of nature, sprung from his own will, he would deprive himself of all hope of the aid he desires." But supposing that the man replied to this, " I accept these consequences, and I am perfectly willing, in fact I should prefer that none should help me when I am in misfortune, so long as it is understood that I need not help them when they are." There is no impossibility, no self-contradiction in this position. What is Kant going to reply?

The fact of the matter is that these passages really give away the whole case. We have here a maxim or principle of action which could be perfectly well made into a universal law, but which as a matter of fact we do not will to be universally observed. If we ask why we do not so will it, the only possible answer is that we do not will it, because it is not right. And as we have seen that such a law could quite easily be universally applied, the inevitable conclusion is that being right means something other and more than being capable of universal application. In the last instance, indeed, Kant by a woeful departure from his principles expressly gives as the reason the fact that the results would be unpleasant to us, thus, in spite of all he has said, putting the reason for our not willing the action in our feelings, in this particular case, in our desire for a certain state of society. But even without this, the case is clear enough. We find that on his own showing, we may think an action not to be right even though it could be universally applied. So that the essence of rightness does not lie in universality, but in something else, whatever it may be. It may be true that we should will to make any right maxim universal. But we should universalize it because it was right, not think it right because it could be universalized.

The point may be emphasized further. Kant says that as rational beings we *could* not will such a course of action to be universal. But why not? As rational beings, we are only concerned with the bare form of universality. Our only reason for not making any rule universal would be that it could not be done, that it would contradict itself. And in these cases the rule would not contradict itself at all. Or we may meet Kant on his own ground and ask how he knows that a rational being could not will such an action to be universal. It certainly does not follow from the conception of a rational being. A rational being simply *qua* rational can will anything so long as it is possible to do so consistently, so long as it does not contradict itself. In this case there is no contradiction. And if in spite of this we do not will it or think it right, the reason must lie in something else not in the nature of reason as such nor in the bare form of universality. Defenders of Kant, such as the translator of the work under discussion, Dr. T. K. Abbott, who argues that he only meant to give a negative test,[1] really concede the whole point at issue. For if we have only got a negative test, we

[1] As a matter of fact, of course, we have seen that his principle gives us no practical test at all, not even a negative one.

cannot have discovered the essential nature and the real meaning of goodness. At best we have only discovered one of its symptoms, some fact about it which follows from its essential nature. But what we set out to look for has not been discovered, and the whole search has to begin over again.

Kant, then, has not succeeded in the task he set himself. He thought that the nature of goodness or rightness could be derived from the conception of a rational being. If, as we have seen to be the case, his attempt thus to derive it was unsuccessful, the reason must be sought in one or both of two possible directions. On the one hand, it may be that he had not really understood what was involved in the nature of a rational being. On the other, he may have been mistaken in thinking that it was connected in this way with the conception of goodness or rightness. It would be well, perhaps, if we want to see which alternative to accept, to examine the conception of rational being a little more closely.

A rational being, of course, is a being endowed with reason. But what is reason? Whatever else it is, it is in the first place a cognitive faculty of the conscious being, it is something in us which enables us to know something. We shall probably best distinguish it from other cognitive faculties by the kind of object that we know by it. Kant would say, for instance, that reason was that which enabled us to know universal and necessary truths. But however we distinguish it, the important point is that it is a form of knowing. As applied to actions, it tells us facts about the actions, it tells us the kind of action each one is. And we are here face to face with the crucial question, "Can reason be practical?" Or, in other words, "Can a knowledge of the nature of an action by itself move us to take that action?" Kant thought that it could: it is essential to his whole position. And if he is wrong in this, we have discovered the fundamental fallacy of his theory.

Let us try to realize the point of view of those who would

hold that on this fundamental point Kant was wrong. We may, to begin with, set against Kant's view the dictum of Aristotle, The intellect by itself moves nothing, has no motive force. Or, in other words the mere knowing that an action, or anything else, is of such-and-such a kind cannot possibly move us to act.

The point is of such vital importance that we must elaborate this point of view a little further. In the elementary stages of reflection, it might seem to us that this was obviously at variance with certain observable facts. We say that the would-be criminal knows that if he commits a murder, he will be hanged. This knowledge is enough to make him refrain from doing so, however much he may want to. I know, when I am ill, that a certain medicine will make me well, and therefore I take it, however unpleasant it may be. Here we have cases of knowledge moving us to action. The argument is really a very superficial one, and only worth mentioning because it helps to illustrate and emphasize the view against which it is directed. For the point is, of course, that it is not the mere knowledge that moves us to action at all. If the criminal did not mind being hanged, if I am absolutely indifferent whether I get well or not, then the knowledge would have no effect on our action one way or another. The reason why the knowledge moves us to action is that it is the knowledge that that particular kind of action will have an effect that we want or desire. But the bare knowledge that a particular action is of a certain kind or will have a certain effect has no influence on us unless we have an interest in that effect or that kind of action, unless, that is, we have some feeling towards it. In short, action of any kind will not take place without the presence of a desire or some element of feeling or emotion. So that if we were pure reason without any desire or feelings, we should not, as Kant thought, act in a particular way, but we should simply not act at all.[1]

[1] We might express this in Kantian terms by saying that the reason cannot be free in his sense. If our reason acts, it acts according to

If this is true, Kant's fallacy lies in thinking that just the bare knowledge that an action is of a certain kind is sufficient to move us to do that action. Why that may sound plausible, at first hearing, is that when we speak of the kind of action we are apt to include in the meaning of that phrase the effect the action has on us: thus, for instance, we may speak of pleasant and unpleasant actions as being different kinds of actions, though the difference lies not necessarily at all in the actions themselves but simply in the effect they have on us. But Kant, of course, is careful to avoid this confusion. When he speaks of the kind of action, he means simply what the action is in itself, apart from its effects on us or any relation to our feelings.

In the light of this, we can get a clearer view of the place of reason in action and the real meaning of reasonable action. Practical reason will mean for us what it meant for Aristotle, who first used the phrase: that is, the ability to discover what will be the best means to an end which we want to attain. The essence of unreasonable action will lie in doing something which will defeat our own ends: for instance, in doing something in obedience to an immediate desire which will hinder the attainment of something else which we really want more. Practical reason will really be the capacity of finding means to ends.

We can apply the same consideration to the meaning of the term "ends." In that connexion we may recall the passage where Kant argues that all rational beings must be ends in themselves, because each one regards himself as an end. And as they are all rational beings, what holds of one must hold of the others. So that they must all be ends in themselves. However ready we may be to accept the valuable practical consequences that Kant draws from the principle

certain laws of its own nature, no doubt. But to start it acting it needs an efficient cause, just as much as natural objects do, in this case, some form of desire or feeling. So far, therefore, is reason from supplying a possible motive for action, that it cannot itself act without a previous desire or feeling to set it in motion.

we should probably all feel that the argument as it stands is singularly unconvincing. And, in the light of the above consideration, we begin to see the reason for that. For it becomes clearer that the argument really rests on a confusion about the sort of fact that being an end really is. Being an end is not, in our ordinary use of the term, a fact about things like being a human being or being green or being a triangle, a fact about the thing itself, a fact which belongs to the thing in its own right. Being an end is not really a fact about the thing at all. My end in ordinary speech means my object or purpose, what I am aiming at or trying to get at or want or desire. It is made an end by being wanted, and if I cease to want it it ceases to be my end. If no one wants it any longer, it ceases to be an end at all. That is, there is strictly no such thing as an end in itself unless we are going to attach an entirely new meaning to the word. Being an end implies some relation to the desires or purposes of some conscious being : and a thing is made an end by this relation. It follows, then, that nothing can be just an end : it could only be an end for someone, the purpose or desire of some conscious being. And there would, of course, be nothing self-contradictory in the view that each conscious being might have a different end, or that the same thing might be an end for one being and not for another.

The same consideration, would apply, surely, to a conception like that of value. We should ask whether value must not be value for someone, whether we do not find that, if we are to think of value at all, we must think of it as essentially related to our feelings or the feelings of some conscious being or beings. This, at any rate, is our ordinary use of it. And ultimately we shall begin to ask ourselves whether we may not be finally forced to say the same of a wider conception like that of good. If we are, we shall have to say that our conception of good necessarily contains in itself a reference to some conscious being. We shall not be able to allow any such ideas as that of good, which was just good and not good for some being. Good would be found to be essentially related to and in some way dependent on the wishes or desires or feelings of some conscious being.

The Kantian would, of course, object here that Kant had already considered the claims of the desires and feelings and given reasons for rejecting them. In the first place, he had argued that to make goodness depend on desires or feelings, would make it something uncertain and fluctuating, because some people might desire a thing and others not, or the same person might desire it at one time and not at another. This is certainly a weighty objection, and will have to be considered at length later. Here it will suffice to suggest a possible line on which it might be met: that is, if we developed the idea of some end which every conscious being, by its very nature, must and would desire, if it only realized what it was. We shall meet with this conception later. In the second place he had argued that such a view would make what we desired not good in itself but only as a means to an end. Here we can only say that Kant, doubtless largely under the influence of a faulty psychology, seems to fail to realize the possibility or the true meaning of anything being desired purely for its own sake. Finally it would be argued that such a view would not give us a thing good in itself, because its goodness would depend upon something else outside of it, namely, our desire of or feeling towards it. This we should readily admit. And we should reply that we do not and cannot recognize the existence or possibility of any such thing as good in itself in that sense, out of all relation to anything else. It simply has no meaning for us. And if it had, it would make goodness something of no interest or importance to us, and of no possible influence upon our actions.

With this, we really return to the point from which Kant started. We shall remember that one of the assumptions on which he seemed to base his theory was that which was expressed by saying that if a thing is really good, it must be good in itself. If that appealed to us at first as a reasonable statement of our own ordinary ideas, it was only because we had not yet realized what it really meant. When we did realize this, instead of accepting it as a correct starting-point, we should be more inclined to describe it as the fundamental fallacy of Kant, as indeed of many other writers. Goodness, we should say now, is not a quality which belongs to things in themselves, quite apart from their effect on or their relation to us[1] or some conscious being. If it were, it could only be related to us as an object of cognition. And if it were simply an object of cognition, something that we merely knew without having any feeling towards it, it could not move us to action, or indeed be of any practical interest or importance to us at all.

There are many other objections to Kant's view. But if the argument has been correct, we have found his fundamental fallacy in the false assumptions from which he starts. They are really two in number. He starts from the assumption that what is good must be good in itself, apart from all relations to anything else. And in consequence of this he is forced to assume that the mere intellectual apprehension of the fact is sufficient to move us to action. The other assumptions which we have ascribed to him follow from these two or are different forms which they take. But, if our argument has been at all correct, we must maintain against this that the simple intellectual apprehension, the bare knowledge of anything can never move us to action. And consequently his idea of a good in itself is incompatible with one of the most deeply recognized characteristics of the moral fact, namely, that it is somehow a reason for action.

[1] Of course, in a sense, as we have seen, Kant does make goodness related to us, because it is an essential quality of rational beings. But that merely means that we, in so far as we are rational, are the things which have this quality. It is obviously a very different thing from asserting that goodness itself consists in a relation to us or to any conscious being. And nothing short of this will satisfy the above criticism.

CHAPTER V

THE KANTIAN FALLACY IN OTHER FORMS

NO one, except his immediate disciples, has attempted to take over and defend Kant's system in all its details. No later writer of any importance has accepted the proposition that goodness simply means universality, in Kant's sense.[1] But, as we have seen, that theory is only the result of a more fundamental error. And this fundamental error, as we shall find, re-appears in many different forms in later writers. The fatal objection to the theory is that it fails to fulfil one of the fundamental conditions of any correct account of the moral fact. Whatever goodness is, it is at least in some way a reason for action, a reason for pursuing those things where it is present and avoiding those where it is absent. And any account of it which fails to show why it should be a reason for action, still more an account which describes it in such a way that it could not possibly be a reason for action, stands condemned. We have now to emphasize this point by a brief consideration of some other ethical theories which are guilty of the same fault and against which the same criticisms are valid.

Let us consider first the work of a living author, whose views are in all their details widely different from those of Kant, although, as we shall see, they rest upon the same fundamentally false assumptions. The theory under consideration was put forward some seventeen years ago by Mr. G. E. Moore in his book *Principia Ethica*. His view is, to put it briefly, that goodness, the primary moral fact, is a simple, indefinable quality, which belongs to some things and not to others, and which can only be perceived directly.

[1] In a different sense of the word " universality," the proposition would be maintained by more than one later writer, for instance, Benedetto Croce.

THE KANTIAN FALLACY IN OTHER FORMS

It is not a complex thing, and it is not a relation to anything else, human feelings or consciousness, for instance. He illustrates the kind of thing he means by the example of a colour, say yellow. We know what yellow is, simply by being directly aware of it. We can say that certain things are yellow, and we can say that the objects which are yellow also have certain other properties, for instance, that they produce a certain kind of vibration in the light. But this is not saying what yellow is. That we simply have to recognize, and we cannot describe it or define it any further. And goodness is a quality of this kind. This is the view that we have now to consider. And in our consideration of it we shall find reason to maintain (1) that Mr. Moore nowhere succeeds in proving that goodness is such a simple, indefinable quality, (2) that, as a matter of fact, he often himself talks about it in a way that clearly implies that it is not, and (3) that such an account of it would be open to the same fatal objections as Kant's theory.

(1) There is really very little attempt at a direct proof that goodness is of this nature. He argues that there must be such simple and indefinable qualities, and this argument we need not contest, although it would certainly not be universally accepted. We want to know whether goodness is one of these qualities, supposing them to exist. And so far as he tries to show this at all, he does it by an attempt to show the impossible consequences which follow from trying to define it. One of his arguments is that the different definitions of it do not agree, and that it is impossible to argue in favour of our own definition and against another except by assuming the definition that we set out to prove. " If," he writes, " good is *defined* as something else, it is then impossible either to prove that any other definition is wrong or even to deny such definition " (p. 11). It is not very easy to see the force of this argument. It is difficult to see why it should apply particularly to goodness more than to anything else, and why the argument should not be used to

prove that not only a definition of goodness but a definition of anything at all was impossible. But in any case the difficulty is an entirely unreal one. If the situation with regard to our knowledge of the moral fact is as described above in our introduction, there is no difficulty in understanding how we come to have different opinions about the correct definition of goodness, nor how we could rationally discuss and argue about the subject.

His other argument on the subject is more serious. He argues (p. 15), " that whatever definition be offered, it may be always asked, with significance, of the complex so defined, whether it is itself good." What we have defined, therefore, cannot be goodness itself, but simply something which is or may be good. Thus, if we define, for instance, goodness as being desired in a certain way, yet we shall see that we cannot really mean this as a definition, we cannot mean that goodness simply is being desired in this way, because we can ask and attach some meaning to the question, " Is it good to desire things or a thing in that particular way ? " But let us apply the argument a little further. Suppose we ask, " Who was that man in the black overcoat I saw going round the corner just now ? " and someone tells us, " Oh, that was our friend Smith." Presumably Mr. Moore would say, " He cannot mean that the man in the black overcoat and Smith are identical, because you can still, with significance, ask the question, ' Was Smith the man in the black overcoat I saw going round the corner ? ' " Of course, the reason why you can still ask the question, and mean something by it is because there is still some doubt. And that is also the only reason why, after suggesting a definition of goodness, you can still ask, " of the complex so defined whether it is itself good." When you ask that question, you are still thinking of goodness as that vague and undefined something which it was to you before you began your speculation about its real nature ; and if you ask that question, it means that you have not yet made up your mind about accepting the definition. Once you have accepted it and have definitely made up your mind that that is what goodness means, there is no longer any meaning in the question at all, whatever Mr. Moore may say.

(2) In several passages Mr. Moore uses other phrases as equivalent in meaning to the term " good " or " goodness." Thus he says (p. 17), " Whenever he thinks of ' intrinsic value ' or ' intrinsic worth,' or says that a thing ' ought to exist,' he has before his mind the unique object—the unique property of things—which I mean by ' good.' " Here goodness is the same as value or worth. In another passage (p. 100), he commits himself more positively to a definition, when he says " that a thing should be an ultimate rational end means, then, that it is truly good in itself." In other words, goodness and being a rational end are identified. And just before this he seems to suggest that the goodness of a thing is a reason for aiming at it, and that to say that there is a reason for aiming at a thing is the same thing as to say that it is good. Thus he writes (p. 99), " The only reason I can have for aiming at ' my own good,' is that it is *good absolutely* that what I so call should belong to me. . . . But if it is *good absolutely* that I should have it, then everyone else has as much reason for aiming at *my* having it, as I have myself." And elsewhere he seems to identify " being good " and " being worth while doing."

Now, can Mr. Moore seriously maintain that the thing which is meant by all these phrases that he uses as equivalent to " good " is a simple and indefinable quality ? Does, for instance, " rational end " convey to anyone a simple idea, incapable of further analysis and definition ? As a matter of fact, the ordinary meaning of saying that a thing is an end is that someone wants it and is aiming at it. But this is just what Mr. Moore does not mean by it. Yet, surely, if he means anything by it, the meaning that it has for him must have some connexion with the other and ordinary meaning, else why does he use the same word ? If it means nothing more than this simple indefinable quality, for which we already have the quite satisfactory name of goodness, it seems an extraordinarily pointless proceeding to introduce another phrase for it which tells us nothing new.[1] The same considerations apply to the use of the term "value." One meaning of value, at any rate, as in Economics, is the capacity of satisfying human wants and desires. Why should we introduce a term that has this meaning into the consideration of a simple, indefinable quality, which has nothing to do with this? Similarly with the idea of goodness as being the reason for aiming at a thing. One reason, at any rate, for aiming at anything is that we want it. But goodness does not mean this. Is, then, goodness merely one member of a class of reasons for action? If we say this, we are getting dangerously near to giving a definition of it, for we have already given its genus. All these considerations suggest that Mr. Moore really finds it difficult himself to think consistently of goodness as a simple, indefinable quality, and is being constantly compelled without realizing it, by the force of facts to introduce some other elements into his idea of it.

(3) This brings us to our positive objections to the view. As we have just seen, Mr. Moore is compelled to say that the goodness of a thing must be thought of as a reason for aiming at it. But on his theory how can this be so? How can it be a motive for action? We are told that it is a simple quality which we perceive immediately. But our mere cognition of it cannot move us to action. Of course, Mr. Moore is not in Kant's unfortunate position of being compelled to say that if we do the action because we desire it, it

[1] The discussion of the idea of " end " in Mr. Moore's article on Teleology in the *Dictionary of Philosophy and Psychology*, to which he refers us in his introduction, really tells us nothing further. His argument there simply amounts to the assertion that certain writers have, as a matter of fact, identified the meanings of " end " and " good." But the whole question is, What does this identification imply? And our view would maintain that to identify the two really implies that goodness in some sense is the same thing as being wanted or desired.

ceases to be good. On his theory, we can perfectly well desire the good, and therefore act so as to attain it. But it is the desire for it which moves us to action, and not at all the goodness of it. The goodness of it and our desire for it are two entirely different things and have no necessary connexion. It becomes, therefore, merely a matter of taste whether we desire what possesses this simple, indefinable quality or not, just as it is whether we like a particular colour or not. The mere fact of a thing being good can never by itself influence us to aim at it or move us to action. In fact, it is not necessarily of any interest to us at all. And this is equivalent to saying that goodness, so far from being a reason for aiming at the things which possess it, can never in any intelligible sense be a reason for action at all. So that Mr. Moore's account of it fails to fulfil one of our essential conditions, just as Kant's does, and for the very same reasons.

There are other objections to the view. For instance, it may well be asked why, if goodness is a simple, indefinable quality which is perceived directly, there can be any doubt or dispute about the matter ? How can anyone fail to see that it is of this nature ? Why do people still go on thinking that they can define it, even after they have read *Principia Ethica* ? Nobody tries to define yellow, in this sense, still less do they dispute about what yellow means. But though it is difficult to see how Mr. Moore could explain these facts, that is not the real, decisive objection to his view. The decisive objection is, to expand what we have already said, that if goodness is such a simple, indefinable quality, we are faced with two alternatives. Either the goodness of a thing can, in itself, afford no possible motive for our aiming at that thing, or else we must say that simple intellectual recognition of the presence of this quality is sufficient to move us to action. Neither alternative, as we have already seen, can we possibly accept.

This same fallacious mode of thinking reappears constantly in the most unexpected quarters. We find it, for instance, in the work of a writer who is sometimes represented as advocating views which are the very antithesis of Kant's, namely John Stuart Mill. Of course, Mill is not consistent even in this fallacy. But it comes up in a curious way in several passages of his *Utilitarianism*.

It is, perhaps, hardly necessary to summarize the argument of this famous work. But we may briefly recall the main points, in so far as they illustrate his commission of this fallacy. It will be remembered that his main thesis is that the only thing absolutely good in itself is pleasure or happiness —he identifies the two—and by this he means not the pleasure of a particular man but the general pleasure, the greatest happiness of the greatest number. In other words, the final good is that as much pleasure as possible should exist in the world. And he attempts to prove this by the assertion that every man desires his own pleasure.

It has often been pointed out that, so far from this latter statement proving the first, it positively contradicts it. For the greatest pleasure of one particular man may often be incompatible with the existence of the greatest amount of pleasure in the world, and is rarely, if ever, absolutely coincident with it. So that if he can only desire his own pleasure, he need not and very often cannot desire the greatest pleasure of the greatest number. But it is more interesting to try to guess why Mill thought that the one fact, if it was a fact, could be taken as a proof of the other. And we can only suppose that it was because he had, at the back of his mind, this idea of goodness as a simple quality which belonged to certain objects in their own right quite apart from any relation to us. If, therefore, we recognize that pleasure, in the case where we know it best, namely, in our own experience of it, always has this quality, it is quite rational to suppose that this quality always and necessarily belongs to it. The argument, then, would be closely analogous to Kant's argument that rational beings are ends in themselves. Unfortunately for Mill, he also had in his mind the idea of goodness

THE KANTIAN FALLACY IN OTHER FORMS 59

not as a quality of objects, but as a relation of objects to us or to conscious beings. That is, he was at the same time thinking of goodness as being identical with being desired. So that he commits the absurdity, from his point of view, of taking the fact that we desire pleasure as a proof that pleasure is good.[1] And with this he destroys his own argument.

We find the same idea in his mind in his curious chapter on the Sanctions of Utilitarianism. The sanction of any rule of conduct, as he explains, is the motive from which it is obeyed. The Sanctions of Utilitarianism mean, therefore, the motives which we have to pursue the greatest happiness of the greatest number. And he explains that our motives for doing so are of various kinds, external, such as fear of punishment, or internal, such as the feeling of discomfort that comes from not doing so, which we call conscience. But the significant thing about the chapter is the fact itself that he has to search for motives, and incidentally also that he thinks of them under the form of the legal idea of Sanctions. For that suggests that the motive for pursuing this thing which is good is to be found in something altogether outside its goodness, and in something which in no way necessarily follows from its goodness. He never suggests, indeed, that the mere fact that the greatest happiness of the greatest number is good could be taken as a motive for pursuing it. He gets, perhaps, nearer to this when he speaks of conscience as "a pain . . . attendant on the violation of duty." But he seems to think of this as a feeling, which we may or may not have, not in any way necessarily connected with goodness, and still less as that which constitutes it or that by which it could be defined. He speaks of it, in fact, as just one of the sanctions, on a level with the external sanctions, all of which are entirely extrinsic to the goodness of good actions and good ends.

Some subsequent forms of Utilitarianism, by avoiding the

[1] I do not wish to suggest that this idea is necessarily an absurdity, but only that it becomes such when used as it is by Mill.

confusions of Mill, make even clearer their dependence upon this false assumption. Of these we need only consider Sidgwick, who adopts the Utilitarian view that the ultimate good thing, the end at which we all ought to aim is pleasure or happiness, the greatest happiness of the greatest number, while utterly rejecting Mill's absurd attempt to prove this by the assertion of the psychological theory that everyone desires only his own pleasure. Sidgwick indeed, combines the Utilitarian doctrine of what the thing is of which we can ultimately predicate goodness, with the doctrine already considered that the quality, goodness, itself is something simple and indefinable which we can only recognize directly. And his exposition is of particular interest because he is one of the few modern authors who frankly recognize that this obliges him to say that the mere intellectual apprehension of this can move us to action. " I imply," he says in language curiously reminiscent of Kant, " that in rational beings as such this cognition gives an impulse or motive to action." (*Methods of Ethics*, p. 35.)

Unfortunately, though he recognizes that many, if not most, people would deny the possibility of this, he nowhere attempts to prove it, or to consider any of the difficulties in the way of it or the revolutionary denial of the evidence of our own experience that it involves. In his only attempt at argument on the subject, he promises to show that any attempt to explain the moral fact in a way which does not involve this fails to do justice to its essential characteristics which we should all recognize. Even that would perhaps hardly be sufficient to convince us of the possibility of something which the evidence of our experience tells us to be impossible. But when we look at his argument on this point we find that it merely consists in an argument that where we call anything good we do not simply mean that we have (actually at the time) a certain feeling towards it, nor that it is merely the command of a certain being or beings. Both these propositions may, of course, be readily admitted without in the least invalidating our criticisms of the idea of goodness as a simple quality, since the alternatives given obviously do not nearly exhaust the possible rival accounts.

Sidgwick, however, is much too critical and fair-minded a thinker to leave the account there. He is obviously not satisfied with a complete divorce of the quality of goodness from the relation of being desired by some conscious being or beings. And thus we find him saying of goodness (p. 106), "We can indicate its relation to desire and choice by giving as its equivalent the term 'desirable.'" Of course, if "desirable" simply means "what ought to be desired," or in other words, "what is good to desire," it tells us nothing more, and is indeed a kind of circular definition. But Sidgwick is not trying to trick us into accepting an identical proposition as an intelligent statement. He tries to explain further the meaning of desirable. "What I recognize as desirable for me I conceive as something which I either do desire (if absent) or should desire if my impulse were in harmony with reason." And he gives us as a final summing-up (p. 108), "I cannot, then, define the ultimately good as desirable otherwise than by saying that it is that of which we should desire the existence if our desires were in harmony with reason."

Here again we get this term "reason" used in a strange and perplexing sense. What meaning can we attach to the phrase, "our desires being in harmony with reason"? One obvious meaning would be that our desires should not conflict or contradict. The clearest case of an unreasonable desire would be a desire the satisfaction of which would hinder us from the attainment of something else which we really wanted more. But this meaning would not seem to meet Sidgwick's requirements, and we must hazard another suggestion. Reason, whatever else it may be, is at least a cognitive faculty, something by which we know facts or truths. To act reasonably, then, would seem to suggest, in its most general sense, to act with knowledge. And our desires being in harmony with reason would mean that we know fully what it is that we desire, what the real nature of the object of our desire is. That which we should desire if our desires were in harmony with reason now becomes that which we should desire if we really knew what it was like. And, on Sidgwick's definition of " good " or " desirable," we must say that when we say that anything is good we simply mean that we should desire it if we really knew all about it and realized what sort of a thing it was.

We are, now, a long way from the original idea of goodness as a simple and indefinable quality. But, rather perhaps, to our surprise, we shall find that Sidgwick is not altogether disinclined to go this distance with us. He considers an attempted definition of goodness, somewhat on these lines only more elaborately expressed, and by no means rejects it unconditionally. The whole passage is worth quoting (p. 108) : " To avoid this objection, it would have to be said that a man's ' true good ' is what he would desire on the whole if all the consequences of all the different lines of conduct open to him were actually exercising in him an impulsive force proportioned to the desires or aversions which they would excite if actually experienced. So far as I can conceive this hypothetical object of desire, I am not prepared to deny that it would be desirable in the sense which I give to the term ; but such a hypothetical composition of impulsive forces involves so elaborate and difficult a conception, that it is surely paradoxical to say that this is what we *mean*, when we talk of a man's ' good on the whole.' " Opinions might differ whether the conception really was so elaborate and difficult. But even if it was, that would not justify Sidgwick's conclusion. For the argument really rests on a failure to realize the exact sense in which we can say that we really mean something or anything by the use of the word " good." The question has been discussed already and there is no need to go into it again. But we may note that Sidgwick's objection might apply, with greater or lesser force, to almost any case of definition. The zoologist for instance, in defining any species of animal would probably use terms which would appear very elaborate and difficult to the ordinary man, who had always been accustomed to talk about this particular sort of animal as something perfectly familiar to him. But that would not in the least invalidate the definition.

To return to the main argument, we find that Sidgwick's position is open to all those objections that we have already considered. But we find also that he, like Mr. Moore, is not really completely satisfied with his own position, and is unable to hold it consistently himself.

We find, then, if our argument is well founded, that it is impossible to consider the moral fact as simply a quality which belongs to certain things, because that would necessitate the further assertion that the mere cognition of this was able to move us to action. And this we declared to be impossible. We have considered the systems of some thinkers which are clearly open to this objection. Others are less clear and more ambiguous on the matter. Butler, for instance, in many ways one of the acutest of philosophers, leaves us in doubt about how exactly he thinks of the moral fact of which his principle of conscience tells us. Rightly understood he holds that conscience prescribes exactly the same actions as enlightened self-love does. But the full significance of this and the exact relation between these two he leaves in obscurity. It can hardly be mere accident that their commands exactly coincide. And there is, at any rate, nothing inconsistent in his account with the view that this principle of reflection in reason, which he calls conscience, is really the intellectual consciousness that certain actions will or will not conduce to our own interest which is what we really desire, He does not explicitly put the question,[1] but we should have to put it

[1] At times he seems to come very near to a definite subordination of conscience to enlightened self-love, as in the famous passage in Sermon XI : " When we sit down in a cool hour, we can neither justify to ourselves this or any other pursuit, till we are convinced that it will be for our happiness or at least not contrary to it." The last clause however, rather weakens the effect of the whole passage.

both to him and to any other system, which left the answer to it in doubt.

So far, then, we have found insuperable objections to supposing goodness, or whatever we are going to call the moral fact, to be a simple quality of certain things. The other alternative is that it is not a quality at all, but a relation to ourselves or to some conscious being or beings. One form of such a view would be a consistent Hedonism which asserted that to say anything was good simply meant that it produced pleasure in us or in someone. Another form would assert that being good meant being desired, in some sense or in some way, either actually or hypothetically under certain conditions. The quotation from Sidgwick given above indicates one form such a doctrine might take. We have now to consider the work of a thinker who did actually maintain such a view, and developed it consistently and in detail. We turn, then, to the *Ethics* of Aristotle.

PART II

ARISTOTLE AND THE GOOD AS PURPOSE

CHAPTER VI

ARISTOTLE AND THE ETHICS (I)

WHEN we begin the study of Aristotle, we seem to enter into a different atmosphere altogether. We are dealing with different modes of thought, different terms, different assumptions. And the first necessity is to realize the real meaning and importance of these differences.

Our first and most obvious difficulty is the difference of language. Kant, of course, wrote in German and not in English. But, when we consider the closeness of the two languages and also the fact that our modern philosophical vocabulary has been formed very largely under Kant's influence, we shall not expect that to be a very formidable hindrance. Even if we cannot read the German, a good translation will give us almost always an exact equivalent in English of the important phrases and passages. But with translations from the Greek, it is quite different. The two languages are much wider apart, and we shall find, which will enormously increase our difficulties, that the important Greek word or phrase has hardly ever an exact English equivalent. For we must remember, that in every language a word or a phrase conveys a great deal more than the one simple idea. It has this bare minimum of meaning; but it has also a whole background of associated or suggested ideas, which together form its full meaning. Now this background of associations may be entirely different in two languages, even when the bare minimum of meaning is the same. And in Greek and in English it very often is so, which makes the task of translating from one to the other very difficult, and sometimes, indeed, impossible. Of course, in cases of simple narrative or description, as for instance, in most historical work, this does not appear much; in general, they deal with simple, concrete facts which are the same everywhere, and of which we only need to know the bare minimum of meaning. But it comes out particularly strongly in poetry and philosophy, though for different reasons. In poetry a great deal of the sensuous effect depends upon the particular associations that the different words have for us, for instance, the particular picture they call up before us. And the English word rarely, if ever, has quite the same associations as the Greek word for which it is used. In philosophy a great deal of the work consists in the close analysis of the exact meaning and all the implications of certain words and phrases. Now, of course, in a Greek book the author is analysing the meaning and implications of a Greek word. But if we read him in English, or even if, reading him in Greek, we translate for ourselves into English as we go along, we cannot help thinking of the author as analysing an English word, which does not have the same implications or exact meaning as the Greek word. That is why, if we read a Greek philosophical work in English, we are so often impressed by a sense of unreality in the argument. And it is why, also, even the best translations must be used with the greatest caution.

Two or three points in which the Greek moral atmosphere or background differed from our own may be briefly suggested here. If we consider our own background of moral assumption, we should recognize that we are apt to think more or less vaguely of morality, or of moral goodness or badness, as a special category of its own, quite distinct from others which we might use in the same connexion. We should incline to think of it as only one among many possible ways of regarding conduct to think of it as right or wrong, or as morally good or bad And we should think of the moral motive as only one among many possible motives for acting, and perhaps, even, as a motive of an entirely different kind from any other. We are ready, therefore to consider the rightness or goodness of an action as something entirely distinct from its pleasantness or desirability or success, or even perhaps opposed to them. And from this attitude of mind we pass easily, with Kant, to the idea of rightness or goodness as a fact about actions, entirely independent of all other facts about them or of their relation to ourselves or to our desires or purposes, or anything else. But to the Greek, on the other hand, such a point of view would seem quite alien and indeed inexplicable. In his ordinary thinking he has little or no tendency to think of morality as something sharply distinguished from the rest of life, or of the moral motive as something different in kind from other motives. In fact, it would hardly be an exaggeration to say that the Greek normally did not think of morality in our sense at all; he did not think of it as something special, with a special province or a special point of view of its own. His natural tendency was much rather to begin by thinking of conduct as a whole.

This difference of outlook has an important result in the influence it exercises on the choice of a starting-point for ethical speculation. Our tendency is, once more, to separate and distinguish morally good or right action from action of other kinds. And we tend particularly to make a sharp distinction between what we want to do, and what we ought to do, between our desires and our duty. The consequence of this is that, as we naturally tend to identify ourselves in questions of action with the desiring or feeling element in us, we are inevitably led to regard morality or duty or moral goodness as something imposed upon us from outside, as laying down something that must be done whether we ourselves want to do it or not.

So that the idea from which we naturally start our moral analysis is the idea of obligation, of something which is binding upon us.

Aristotle, however, begins in quite a different way, as is, indeed, inevitable for anyone starting from the Greek point of view. For in the Greek language there is really no word that means "ought" or "right" in the sense in which we use them to imply the idea of moral obligation. The chief moral term upon which they would naturally start their investigations is the word Agathos, which we translate as "good." Only in so translating it, we are apt to miss its real meaning or at any rate its full implication, and to attach, wrongly, our specifically moral associations to it. The Greek word, as applied to a person, corresponds much more nearly to our use of the term "good" in a phrase like "a good cricketer" or "a good soldier"; that is to say, it means that the person in question does a piece of work or performs a particular function well, or—what is really the same thing from a slightly different point of view—that he does what he sets out to do, fulfils his purpose or attains his end successfully. As applied to a thing, the nearest analogy in English would perhaps be a phrase like "a good piece of work," which similarly has the suggestion of a purpose carried out or an end attained. And that is for the Greek the fundamental meaning of the word which we translate as "good." Thus we find Plato in the *Gorgias* using practically interchangeably two terms which are generally translated as "good" and "useful" respectively. And in the *Ethics* Aristotle does the same thing with phrases which mean "the good" and the "end" or "object." This throws further light on the point already noticed, that the Greek tends, in general, to deal with conduct as a whole, and not from any particular point of view. And one essential thing that he finds underlying all conscious action is purpose, and from this fact he makes his start. So that we may summarize the distinction we have drawn by saying that whereas we naturally tend to begin our moral investigation from the conception of obligation, the Greek would rather start from the far more fruitful conception of purpose.

Of course—the warning should hardly be necessary—this must not be understood as asserting that the Greek even in his most unreflective moments unequivocally identified what is good to do with what we want to do. He had a firm grasp of the fact that what we want to do at any moment is not always or necessarily good. But still it remains true that the reference to purpose, and therefore, in the broadest sense, to desire, was at the back of the mind of the ordinary Greek who used the word which we translate " good." And if he called a purpose or desire bad, we should almost always find that he was implying, more or less consciously, that it hindered the attainment of some other purpose or desire.

One other point, and that of rather a different nature, must be grasped in order to realize the atmosphere in which a Greek thinker would approach the consideration of these problems. Always present to him and colouring his thinking about everything would be his consciousness of the importance of the State. The state, the city community organized politically, was to the Greek omnipresent and concerned in every form of activity that any of its members might undertake. In modern times, we tend rather to identify the state with the government, and to think of it as a body which does certain things for us but stands outside the greater part of our life, so that we only come consciously into contact with it now and again. And there is, in consequence, too often a tendency for us to omit all consideration of the state in our ethical speculation. But to the Greek, who had but one word for " state " or " city," the thought of the state was always present. For him it was the great moral agency, the chief educator: that was, in fact, the object for which it existed. The real justification of anything lies in the moral effect which it produces on individuals, and a thing as powerful and all-embracing as a state must, above all others, be careful that its power is exercised with a view to the moral development of its citizens. The ideal statesman, both for Plato and Aristotle, is not the man who discovers new sources of taxation, or forms wise alliances with foreign states or conducts a successful war, but the man who leaves the citizens better men than he found them. Moral philosophy, therefore, which is the search for the true end of man, is particularly the proper study for statesmen. And the *Ethics* is written throughout with this object in view.

Let us see how Aristotle approaches the question. Like Kant, he essays to begin with some simple, incontestable proposition on which he can base his argument. Kant begins, in his assertion that nothing is absolutely good except a good will, with the statement of a moral judgment which he thinks will find universal acceptance among our moral ideas. Aristotle begins rather with a wider and more general statement which appears to him obviously and undoubtedly true about action as a whole. " Every art and every kind of enquiry, and likewise every act and purpose, seems to aim at some good ; and so it has been well said that the good is that at which everything aims." All conscious action is directed towards some end or good, for he uses the two words interchangeably. And the end or good in its most general sense is simply something that we want. It is the being wanted that makes it an end and therefore a good (see III, iv). So far we have merely had a general statement about all action, right or wrong alike, and there are as yet no grounds for any moral distinction between actions.

But on proceeding we find differences of kind between the ends of different actions (I, i. 2). Thus some actions seem to be their own ends and pursued for their own sake, as when we do anything not for the result we hope to produce but simply, as we should say, for the pure pleasure of doing it. Such, to take perhaps the simplest example, would be certain bodily movements or forms of exercise which we took simply because we liked them. Other actions are done not for their own sake at all, but in order to produce some result, tangible or otherwise, beyond the action. The simplest example of these would be the processes of manufacturing any article, where what was wanted was the article, and the actions were taken simply as a means to producing them. This distinction is important, and will occur again, but for the moment it is of less interest than another distinction, that is the distinction which cuts across the previous one (I, i. 5), between superior and subordinate ends, or between ends which really are ends and pursued for themselves and ends which are really only means to some further end, though for a time and for certain actions they may be thought of as real ends. Thus, to modernize Aristotle's own instance (I, i. 4) the end of the activities of a munition factory may be the production of shells. But the production of shells, is, in its turn, only desired as a means to a further end, the efficient action of the artillery. And that in its turn is really only a means to the final end of all military effort—victory in war. And, for the statesman, victory is only the means to a further end still.

The distinction so far is sufficiently obvious. But now it leads Aristotle on to one of his great fundamental ideas (which he shares, of course, with other Greek thinkers)—the idea of one final end of all action. "If then," he says (I, ii. 1), "in what we do there be some end which we wish for on its own account, choosing all the others as means to this . . . this evidently will be the good or the best of all things." He supposes that we shall find on examination that all human activities are really directed towards one end alone. And, indeed, it is practically necessary to find some one principle on which to co-ordinate and reconcile different and conflicting aims. We cannot really treat all our desires or aims as having equal claims on us, if for no other reason than that they will inevitably at times conflict, and then we have to decide between them and make up our minds what we really want most. So that we must have some principle on which we can decide between them, even if we say that we select that which gives us most pleasure at the moment. For even then we are really assuming one end, namely, the greatest amount of immediate pleasure. We must always be able to get some general idea of what our end is, even if it amounts to no more than this.

The discovery of this end and the application of it when discovered is above all the work of the statesman or ruler, and is indeed the proper subject of the science of politics. It is not so essential for the ordinary private individual to recognize explicitly what the end of man is: he may, and often does, pursue his own end without being fully conscious of its nature. But the statesman has to think for others as as well as for himself, and is constantly faced with the necessity of arbitrating between or reconciling the different aims of the different members of the community. And if the state is, as Aristotle most emphatically believes it to be, the organization above all others whose aim is the education of the citizens and the realization for them of the good life, it is essential that those responsible for the guidance of the state should have a clear and explicit idea of what this good life is. And the knowledge of this is the science of Ethics or Politics, which, for Aristotle as for most Greek thinkers, is the same thing.

We are thus presented with the idea of an end to which all other ends are subordinate. An end being made such by being desired or wished for, the final end is that which we do in some sense, consciously or unconsciously, wish for more than anything else. What is it, then, which all human beings are really aiming at?

In Chapter IV Aristotle faces this question. "As to its name," he says, "I suppose nearly all men are agreed; for the masses and the men of culture alike declare that it is happiness, and hold that to 'live well' or to 'do well' is the same as to be 'happy.'" The Greek word here translated "happiness" has a much more general and extended meaning than its English equivalent.[1] It really means something

[1] Accordingly, henceforward, I shall distinguish the word "happiness" when used as a translation of the Greek word, Eudaimonia, from its use in its ordinary English sense by putting it into inverted commas.

like "well-being": the word "wealth" in its old English sense would perhaps represent it more nearly than anything else. Aristotle, in fact, hardly regards his statement as being anything more than a matter of names. But it is really something more. For, however the word is translated, it means a condition of oneself. And this means, therefore, that each person's end is that he should be in a certain condition, whatever that condition may be: for "they differ as to what this happiness is."

In Chapter V, where Aristotle begins to consider some of these different views, we get an excellent illustration of what he would call the dialectical method of ethical investigation. That method consists in the examination and criticism of ordinary views on the subject: any widespread view must be supposed to have at least some truth in it even if inadequate and incomplete by itself. And by an examination of these views and a realization of their insufficiency or their inconsistency with themselves or with each other, we may hope to be led on to a detection of the truth which is in all of them. This is what he now tries to do.

The idea of pleasure as the end he dismisses at once as degrading: it is obviously inconsistent with our most elementary moral ideas, and cannot be accepted as explaining them. Later he subjects the nature of pleasure to a most careful examination, but for the present its inconsistency with our ordinary moral judgments, is taken as sufficient reason for dismissing it. "Honour" or reputation is treated more carefully, but that too, has to be dismissed. It is a condition not of the person honoured but of the people who honour him: and we cannot think of a condition of other people as our end. We must think of the good as "something that is peculiarly a man's own." But besides this there is a more important point. We observe that a desire for honour is really a desire to be thought good, and we value honour because it makes us think that we are good. It seems, then, that it is only valued as a sign of the presence of goodness or virtue, or excellence, and this suggests that goodness is of more value than it. This consideration explains at once why people come to think of honour as an end and also why we cannot finally accept it as such. Are we then to say that goodness or excellence is the end? This is more plausible, but suffers itself from a contradiction. For if we say that this is good, that it is good to have all our faculties developed to the highest pitch of excellence, then it will follow that it is better to have these faculties developed and to be able to exercise them, than merely to possess them and " to be asleep or inactive " all through life or to be prevented by misfortune from exercising them. This suggests the direction in which we shall eventually look for the answer to our question. But for the present the discussion is still purely critical. The claims of wealth to be the end are dismissed very briefly. Money is obviously desired for what it will bring, not for itself alone.

Omitting the metaphysical arguments in Chapter VI, we come in Chapter VII to the positive examination of the idea of " happiness " itself. He begins his analysis by distinguishing the essential marks of it, the conditions that any description of it must satisfy to be admitted. As the final end, it must be what is chosen for itself: and further than that it must never be chosen for anything else. There are things, of which Aristotle gives instances, which may be desired for themselves, but are also desired as conducing to complete " happiness." But the final end can never be desired for the sake of anything else. It is the most desirable of all things: but not as one among other good things—for then it would be " plain that the addition of the least of other goods must make it more desirable "—but as in itself including them all.

What, then, is it that fulfils these conditions? To answer this, we must ask what is the function of man. The function of anything, of course, is that which it is its nature to do, that which it does better than it does anything else and better than anything or anybody else does. Things may really be defined and classified by their functions: for the function is the active expression of a thing's essential and distinctive characteristics. This may be illustrated by the case of the different professions, or the different organs of the body, which we define and distinguish by stating their function or the work they do. And as all men have a common nature in virtue of which they are identical with each other and different from all other beings, we must suppose a function of man as such. The active exercise of this nature is that which man can do alone, or better than any other being. So that a man performs his function by being most completely a man, by carrying on the activities which are most particularly his. We begin to see, then, the reason for the close connexion which is assumed rather than stated between the end which is wanted and the function. For in performing the function we are being most truly ourselves and doing what it is our nature to do.

Now the real " nature " of any kind of thing is, for Aristotle, to be found in those characteristics which distinguish it from other kinds, rather than in those which it has in common with them. If, therefore, we want to find the nature and the function of man, we must ask what are his special characteristics which distinguish man from other living creatures. And we find this to consist in the presence of reason or a rational element in his nature. And this shows itself in a twofold form. There is the reason itself, the intellectual faculty which apprehends truth, in whatever form. And there is the capacity of reasonable action. This last is something very different from Kant's pure practical reason, purified from all element of feeling or desire. It is the capacity of organizing and co-ordinating our desires and emotions, and controlling or checking the immediate impulses to action so as to enable ourselves to secure what we really want. It is really, in fact, the capacity of acting with a purpose, of suiting and subordinating means to ends, instead of acting from blind instinct or emotional impulse without thought of the results which our action will produce.

The active exercise, then, of his rational nature will be the true function of man. We must add " in accordance with excellence or virtue," though the addition is really hardly necessary. For that the activity should be good or " in accordance with excellence " merely means that it should be most completely itself, that the faculty which is exercised should be developed to its full extent. And we must add " a full term of years " or a complete life, because we need a life which gives full time and opportunity for the development and exercise of these faculties. And thus we get to our final definition of " happiness."

In Chapter VIII Aristotle proceeds to test this definition by comparing it with popular ideas on the subject and showing that it really contains all that is true in them and explains how they come to be held. The important point for us to notice here is his treatment of the idea of goodness or excellence or virtue as the end. He admits its supreme importance, but with the proviso " that it makes no small difference whether the good be conceived as the mere possession of something or as its use—as a mere habit or trained faculty or as the exercise of that faculty." The possession of goodness is different from the use of it; and the latter is in its nature more desirable than the former. It is not enough to have all our qualities and capacities trained and developed up to the highest pitch if we remain passive through life. The very fact of having our faculties so developed will make us want to use them, and we should not be satisfied unless we could do so. We should not, perhaps, even value very greatly the possession of the highest faculties unless they were going to be used. And if we had them we should certainly not be content until we could use them. So in the very nature of things it could never satisfy us merely to be of such a nature. For the mere fact of being so would make us want to act accordingly; and if we were prevented from so acting we could not be completely satisfied; but, on the other hand, it would be equally unsatisfactory if we had to act in that way (or in any way) without being of such a nature. And so we are brought to the full account of the only completely satisfying end, which is to be of a certain character—really, of a completely developed human character—and to be able to act accordingly. It is in the activity proper to our nature that we find the most complete satisfaction.

The one point is really indisputable. Every one would recognize that if a man is of a certain nature he will want to act according to this nature, and will not really be satisfied if he is prevented from doing so. But Aristotle's account contains more than this. For it involves the assertion, not only that if a man's character is developed in a certain way he will want to act in a certain way, but also that he will want his character to be developed in a certain way if it is not so already. But is this true? There certainly seem to be cases, within the experience of every one, where human beings show no perceptible desire to develop their characters on the lines approved by Aristotle, where they seem perfectly content to leave their faculties undeveloped or to develop them in a direction which we could only call evil. It certainly looks at least as if we should have to use the word "want" in a very special sense, if we are going to assert that such people really "wanted" to be good all the time. This question will have to be discussed much more fully at a later stage, but, for the moment, we are concerned to find what answer Aristotle gives to it. And we can only say that he never really faces the question at all. The nearest approach to an answer, perhaps, may be found in a casual phrase used by him in discussing the special problem of pleasure. There he says (VII, xiii, 6), " Yet perhaps they do in fact pursue a pleasure different from that which they fancy they pursue and would say they pursue—a pleasure which is one and the same for all. For all beings have something divine implanted in them by nature." These sentences contain the germ of an important line of thought. But it is not developed by Aristotle himself.

The fact is, perhaps, that the question never really presented itself to Aristotle as it does to us. He is aiming, above all, at giving, as far as possible, a practical guide to the statesman who has to decide what results he wants to produce in developing the character of the members of his state. And as he has to deal with men in the mass, he is more interested in the common qualities of human beings than in the individual characteristics which distinguish them one from another. If the question had been put to Aristotle in this form, he would probably have replied that every man, just in so far as he was human, would wish to develop his distinctively human nature. If a man fully realized what this meant and yet felt no desire at all in this direction, he could really hardly be described as a human being at all. And for the practical purposes of the statesman it would not be possible to take into account such exceptional and abnormal cases.

CHAPTER VII

ARISTOTLE AND THE ETHICS (II)

THE conclusion that reason or the rational element is the true nature of man suggests Kant's proclamation of reason as the supreme good. But the resemblance between the two views is apparent merely, while the differences are fundamental. A consideration of what reason means to Aristotle will bring out the contrast clearly.

Reason is the faculty in us of apprehending truth. And the mere apprehension of a truth or a fact cannot by itself move us to action.[1] But there are two senses in which, if we are careful to see exactly what we mean, we may speak of reason as a motive to action. In the first place the knowledge which reason gives us may itself be an end: we may want to know for its own sake. And, secondly, reason may inform us of the right means to some other end which we already want. In both these cases we exercise this intellectual faculty, and the result it gives us affects our action: in the one case as being itself the object of desire, and in the other as informing us of the means to attain the object of our desire. But in both cases the exercise of this faculty demands a motive of desire to set it working. If it works well, if the faculty in us is properly developed, we possess what Aristotle calls "intellectual excellence." And the whole of Book VI is devoted to an examination of the different forms of intellectual activity and the different kinds of object of which it gives us knowledge. The whole of this exposition is extremely interesting, and deserves careful attention. But the general idea of what "intellectual excellence" is, is sufficiently clear. Our present interest lies rather in another direction. We

[1] See VI, ii. 5.

have in us, of course, many other desires and impulses besides the desire for knowledge. And we want to know how these should be developed and organized, and what the relation of reason to them is. If these are developed and organized in the right way we have what Aristotle calls " moral excellence " or goodness of character. What this consists in exactly and how it should be developed is not so clear. And that is what we now have to examine.

Aristotle asks first whether this good character comes by nature, is inborn in us, or whether it needs training and development. And he answers that we have by nature only the capacity of acquiring it, and that this capacity has to be developed and actualized by training. This answer we shall readily accept. It is, indeed, an obvious fact of experience that our characters are formed and modified by our education and environment. And it is in accord with modern biological theory, which tells us that we inherit little more than the general characteristic of educability, and that the forms this takes depend upon our circumstances and all the influences which these bring to bear on us.

We can only, then, reach a good character at the end and as a result of a period of training of a certain length. And when we have attained a good character, it means that we are of such a nature as to perform good acts spontaneously. In fact, what are called good acts are really only good in the strict sense of the word, if they are performed as the spontaneous result of a good character. And the good character is formed by doing such acts, the sort of acts a good man would do. At the beginning of our life's training we perform such acts under the direction of another, and from other motives than for their own sake, chiefly, no doubt, for the sake of rewards and the fear of punishment. And by doing them we become of such a character as to do them spontaneously. This is the work of education. But it is only possible because there is really there from the beginning some sort of underlying impulse towards the good, because in some sense we "naturally" take pleasure in good acts (for that is almost the definition of good acts). At the beginning of our conscious lives, however, there is no guarantee that this impulse towards goodness will be strong enough to overcome all the other conflicting impulses, desires and passions in us. The rewards and punishments are only used to aid it. And while to begin with we do good acts from these extraneous motives, the fact of doing them often enables us to recognize them as good, and hence to come to desire to do them for their own sakes. We might illustrate this process by the analogy of a pupil at a school who begins to work at any subject for fear of punishment, but may end by developing a real interest for it or by finding the mere exercise of his intellectual power so satisfactory that he works for its own sake. This is, roughly expressed, Aristotle's doctrine of the training of moral goodness.

But what is this moral goodness ? What is the definition, or, at any rate, the test of a good act ? What sorts of action may we take as symptoms of a good character ? And with the answer to this question we are introduced to Aristotle's famous doctrine of the Mean. This is based on the general principle which is taught us by experience, that of most things it is possible to have too much or too little and that we have to avoid excess or defect in them and look for the right amount. And he applies this as a practical test of good actions. The good action is that which avoids the excess or the defect and strikes the mean between them.

Our opinion about the goodness of actions, then, depends on some sort of quantitative estimate. But, of course, we are not to take this quantitative estimate as a matter of physical measurement, although Aristotle's own illustration of it is the right amount of a particular sort of food which it is advisable to eat to keep in good condition. The quantitative estimate applies in the most general sense to tendencies to different kinds of action, in which we do recognize a difference of degree, and the consequent possibility of a too much, a too little, and a right amount. We see this illustrated particularly clearly in our emotions, fear, anger and the like, which impel us to particular kinds of action, and which do admit of degrees of intensity, and consequently of degrees of the extent to which they influence our actions.[1] But we might also apply it in some cases to rules or principles of conduct, to what Kant would call maxims, to which we may pay more or less attention. And the doctrine of the Mean simply lays down that anyone of these tendencies to action may be carried too far or not far enough, and that consequently there is a point at which we can say that it has been carried to just the right degree. And it is this point for which we have to look. The doctrine, in fact, tells us the question that we ought to ask. We are not to ask, that is, simply, Is this a good tendency or a bad one? but rather, How far are we to develop this tendency or give it rein? The doctrine is, of course, the very antithesis of Kant's. We are not, like him, to look for a rule of universal applicability, to ask that the principle of any good action should be universalized. It is a fundamental principle of Aristotle, that such universal rules, which lay down beforehand what sort of actions we must do, are impossible. We ask rather, How far are we to carry this tendency? How far is this rule to be applied? And we have to consider each case on its merits, taking into account all the circumstances. We are not to ask for a universal law that it is right to act in such and such a fashion, but rather we must ask, as Aristotle says, whether we are acting in this fashion " at the right times, and on the right occasions and towards the right

[1] We should, perhaps, distinguish, as Aristotle fails to do, between the strength of the tendency to the emotion, and the strength of the emotion itself when it is actually experienced. The mean applies to both, but more particularly to the former. Thus, in the case of any particular emotion, say, anger, it is primarily a question of the right development of the tendency to feel anger, so that we get angry only on the occasions when we ought to get angry. It is a further question, how angry we ought to be when we are angry; and the right answer to this will vary with the different circumstances of each particular case. As a matter of fact, that the actual emotion of anger should reach the intensity appropriate to the particular case, would be one of the ways in which we should show that the general tendency to anger had been developed to the right degree.

persons and with the right object and in the right fashion." (II, vi. 11).

It is, therefore, of the very nature of the question which we must ask that we cannot answer it in general terms beforehand. Just because all the circumstances have or may have to be taken into account we cannot lay down any rule of universal applicability. And ultimately each case has to be decided by a sort of intuition. "Such matters," as Aristotle says (II, ix. 8), "lie within the region of particulars, and can only be determined by perception." But that is not to say that we are left without any general principle to guide us. We have already been told the point of view from which we are to approach each particular question. But there is more than that. We are not left simply, so to speak, to find any point along the line at which we are to find the Mean. In many cases, at any rate, we are able to fix beforehand the point at which the tendency could clearly be said to pass into excess or to fall into defect, though there may be a considerable area between these points left undetermined. We know, for instance, that we must not be so careful of our lives as to throw away our weapons and fly from battle as soon as there is any danger, nor must we be so ready to go into danger as to risk our lives when there is nothing of any value to be gained by it. And many other practical hints may be given. Aristotle gives us one of particular value when he says (II, ix. 6) that we must always be particularly suspicious of the alternative which is most pleasant to us, and that in case of doubt we shall generally be safe to choose the less pleasant one.[1]

But the great practical value of the doctrine lies really in this—that it calls attention to the point, which would probably be generally admitted, that all, or nearly all, of these tendencies could be carried too far, that almost any moral rule that

[1] This, presumably, only applies while our character is incompletely developed. The man of developed good character finds the greatest pleasure in good actions, and his character cannot be considered completely developed until he does so.

we could formulate would be capable of having a too exclusive attention paid to it, and that the same tendency which, followed up to a certain point, is a virtue may become, by being carried too far, a positive fault. But the truth of this proposition, even when admitted, is too often apt to be forgotten, so it is of the first importance to insist that it ought to be always held in mind.

The practical value of the doctrine may be brought home to us even more clearly by a modern parallel. A modern writer, Mr. Graham Wallas, in his *Human Nature in Politics*,[1] urges the application to political reasoning of what he calls the quantitative method, which is in reality neither more nor less than the doctrine of the Mean with different technical terms and applied rather to practical politics than to morals. The whole point of his argument is that we should, in many cases, at any rate, cease to ask simply whether we want this or that and should ask rather how much of this we want, and how much of that. He suggests that to get a common ground for discussion between the Socialist and the Individualist, we should put the question not Is Socialism right or wrong? but How much Socialism do we want, and how much Individualism? And in a brilliantly written passage he imagines a discussion on " the best size for a debating-hall to be used, say, by the Federal Deliberative Assembly of the British Empire." And he suggests that what would very likely happen would be that we should have one man reiterating that the Parliament Hall of a great empire ought to represent the dignity of its task, and another man answering that " a debating assembly which cannot debate is of no use," whereas the only possible grounds for a practical discussion would be to force both to ask How much dignity? and How much debating convenience? And he recognizes with

[1] In his later book, *The Great Society*, Mr. Graham Wallas explicitly uses the analogy of Aristotle's theory to explain his own views. I may perhaps be permitted a sentiment of mild gratification in reflecting that before the publication of the latter work I had called attention to the resemblance in an article in the *Hibbert Journal*, critical of Mr. Wallas's views.

Aristotle that in the last resort these questions " can only be determined by perception " when he writes: " The political thinker has indeed sometimes to imitate the cabinet-maker, who discards his most finely divided numerical rule for some kind of specially delicate work, and trusts to his sense of touch for a quantitative estimation."

The doctrine of the Mean as Aristotle gives it us is intended to be some sort of practical guide to action. He has said that the good character is formed by doing good actions, or actions such as the good man would do. And at this stage he is only concerned to get some general idea of what sort of actions are of this kind. He does not, therefore, attempt to tell us more than this. He does not attempt to tell us why these actions are good, nor what it is that fixes the right extent to which a tendency is to be developed or allowed free play. It is not merely the fact that it is a mean, that it might be carried further or not so far, nor need we suppose that Aristotle believes that there is any magic in a particular quantity of anything taken by itself. The answer is not, however, very difficult to find. We can only say that the excess begins when one tendency or one rule of action is followed to the exclusion of other tendencies or to the neglect of other considerations. What the doctrine implies is that all these tendencies, all these so-called particular virtues, must be developed harmoniously and none developed at the expense of others. All these tendencies are human tendencies, part of our nature as men, and therefore the complete realization of our human nature demands that they should all be developed as far as possible. But the essential condition for doing this is that none of them should be made an end in itself, or allowed to absorb our attention to the exclusion of the others.

The explanation enables us to understand why it is good to observe the Mean, why—for this is what calling it good really means—we really want to observe the Mean. It is because only by so doing are we able to satisfy to the greatest extent possible all the different tendencies of our nature, and to develop them all to the fullest degree. And it throws a light, too, on Aristotle's idea of reason or the rational element in us, and shows how much wider is his conception of it than Kant's. For Aristotle, the rational element is not something altogether separate and distinct from the feeling element, nor is its development something different from or opposed to the development of the feeling element. For, as thus organizing and unifying our feeling element, it really enables us to develop and satisfy all our desires so far as it is possible to do so harmoniously, so that the development of this higher element really includes the fullest possible development of the lower.

But we must always remember that this doctrine of the Mean is only intended to be of limited application, and Aristotle himself warns us of the danger of misunderstanding and misapplying it. It only applies to our particular tendencies or desires, and indeed not to all of these. The development of our intellectual faculties and the desire for truth, for instance, are not things of which we could have too much. To apply the Mean to that would necessitate saying that there were occasions on which it was better to be in ignorance or in error about something, and such an assertion, for Aristotle at any rate, would be too absurd even to be discussed. It only applies, as we have already seen, in the domain of " moral excellence " or goodness of character, and in this only to the particular elements of goodness. He expressly warns us against regarding virtue or goodness as itself a thing of which we must have a mean or right amount. It is not, that is to say, a thing of which it is possible to have an excess. And the desire for goodness or happiness, the impulse which drives us towards our final end, is not a feeling which can be felt too strongly or have too much attention paid to it. Only to attain this final end we have to organize and harmonize our particular desires and purposes and feelings in the light of the doctrine of the Mean.

But even in applying it to these particular tendencies

there is great need for care and risk of misunderstanding. We may find ourselves taking a tendency to a kind of action which is itself an excess or defect and trying to find a mean, or a right amount of this. Thus, we may say that we have a tendency or impulse on going into action to throw away our arms and bolt. But are we to try to find a mean of this tendency? Are we to ask when and under what circumstances it is right to act in this way? Obviously not, because it is never right to do so. And the reason is that this tendency is only a particular form, in this case an excess, of a more general tendency, namely, to preserve our own lives and avoid danger, which tendency carried to the right extent, at the right time, in the right place and circumstances, is good.

We seem to need, then, some sort of classification and description of the different tendencies to action in our nature, establishing which are the more fundamental or general ones admitting of excess, defect, or a mean, and which are particular forms, excesses or defects or the right amount, of them. And this Aristotle tries to give us in the account of the particular virtues to which he devotes the second half of Book III, and the whole of Book IV. But it may be said at once that this is one of the least satisfactory parts of his account. The list of the particular virtues which he gives us, taken as it is largely from a purely conventional popular classification, is of little or no value. They are not all co-ordinate tendencies of the same kind, on a level with one another. We shall find, if we examine them, that some are more fundamental than the others, or that some are merely different forms or manifestations of some more elementary impulse.[1] We need some much more scientific classification. And if we are anxious to apply Aristotle's principles in a more satisfactory way, we might hope to get help in the attempt from modern psychological investigation, which attempts to classify our instincts and emotions and to make a distinction between the primary and secondary, or the

[1] Occasionally his description is simply absurd, as when he describes truthfulness as the mean between exaggeration and understatement.

simple and compound forms. A good deal of work of this kind has been already done. And, whether successful or unsuccessful, it is thoroughly in the spirit of Aristotle, and the attempt would have to be made if we wished to work out his principles in a satisfactory way.

The whole doctrine of the Mean may be well illustrated by the analogy which Aristotle himself draws (II, vi, 9) between the good character and a work of art, a statue or a picture, of which we say " that nothing could be taken from it or added to it " without spoiling it. Anything added would have to be added to one part and would increase that part out of proportion to the rest, and so spoil the symmetry of the whole. And the analogy would help us to meet the charge sometimes brought against the doctrine, that Aristotle makes merely a quantitative distinction between virtue and vice. This would be true if we considered each individual virtue in isolation from the others. If we looked at this one tendency alone, we might say, when it had become an excess, that there was merely more of it or that it had become stronger. The difference in that tendency alone is one of quantity or degree of intensity. But the difference in the whole man is decidedly qualitative. The balance or proportion of his nature is upset, and his character has become different in kind. It is exactly analogous to what would happen to a beautiful statue, if we suddenly made one limb double its proper size. If we looked at that limb alone, we might say merely that it was larger. But the whole, now that its proportion is upset, has suffered a qualitative change. It has lost its positive quality of beauty, and become grotesque. That is the answer to this objection. But the objection itself really arises from the error we have already been warned against, of not realizing the limits of the application of the doctrine of the Mean and thinking that it claims to tell us more than it really does.

Having thus given us a general idea of what goodness or excellence of character is, Aristotle next proceeds to ask in

Book III under what conditions this can be shown in action. Under what conditions can we say that an action expresses a man's character, and therefore can be called good or bad and praised or blamed accordingly? Or, more especially, what kind of actions can we call good, and regard as the result and symptom of a good character?

To be good, an action must in the first place be voluntary, or, as perhaps the word would be better translated, willing. This implies something more than the mere absence of physical compulsion, and really almost amounts to saying that the action must be one in the doing of which we feel pleasure. At any rate, it is not completely voluntary or willing if we feel pain in doing it. But more than this is necessary. To be completely good an action must be not only willing but also the result of something which is variously translated choice or purpose or decision or will. This is described by Aristotle largely by contrasting it with other things which it is not. It is not wish, because wish is for the end while " choice " is of the means, or more exactly—for there is no single Greek word equivalent to our word " means "—of the things which conduce or contribute to the end. " Choice " is also of the actions immediately in our power, which lie there before us to be done at once. And it is opposed to our immediate impulses or passions because it is deliberate and acts after deliberation. Deliberation is that intellectual process which shows us the right steps up to a desired end.

As a description of specifically good actions, this account is open to a serious objection. For it seems to apply rather to actions which are taken simply as a means to an end, and which have no value in themselves. We must remember that " happiness " is the end, a good character exercising itself in good actions. And we seem to have a distinction between two classes of actions. On the one side, there are the actions which are done simply as a means to an end, merely with a view to developing a good character which is not yet formed, or, when it is formed, with a view to removing external difficulties in the way of its unimpeded exercise. These actions are not really good themselves or are good only by analogy, and yet it is to these that " choice " and the process of deliberation as defined by Aristotle seems particularly to apply. But on the other hand, when we have developed the good character, when we have removed external objects to its exercise, and are acting freely " in accordance with excellence," we can hardly describe our activity as concerned with means to ends at all. Our actions are the direct result of a formed character, and are willed, as Aristotle himself says, for their own sakes. These are the only actions which are, in the strictest sense, good. And yet the distinction of means and ends has really disappeared in them, and with it apparently the processes of deliberation and " choice."

Aristotle does not deal with this point, and does not even clearly express this distinction. And in consequence he does not draw the distinction between, to use J. S. Mill's phrase, desiring things as a means to happiness and desiring them as a part of happiness. If we realize what that means, we shall see that even when we have reached the final stage of development we still act from deliberate choice or purpose, though in a different way from that in which we acted when it was simply a question of discovering the right means to an end. Each of these really good actions is in a sense a part of " happiness," but none of them alone is the whole of " happiness," and further if it was treated as such it might become an excess and so cease to be good. And the sense in which they are done from deliberate choice is that they are done with full realization of their true nature, that each one is a partial realization of " happiness," but only a partial one. The action of this sort is " chosen " or " purposed " in so far as it is fully self-conscious, done with a full realization of its nature and its place in the whole scheme of activities, done because it is felt as part of the whole. And in that sense we should probably all agree that **the truly good action must be the result of deliberate choice.**

CHAPTER VIII

ARISTOTLE AND THE ETHICS (III)

THERE are two points in Aristotle's argument, which are not really questions essential to his main doctrine, but which deserve a brief mention, before we pass on to his final position. The first is his treatment of the phenomenon of "incontinence" as it is conventionally translated, though it would be better expressed by the English phrase "weakness of will." What are we to say of the man who knows what is right and really wants to do it, and yet on particular occasions cannot resist desires or impulses to do what he knows is wrong?

This was a burning question for Greek ethical speculation: and Aristotle starts his considerations of it by an examination of the suggestions of his predecessors. It is, indeed, easy to see why the question is of particular interest for Aristotle, as for Greek thought generally. For to him to know what is right and to want to do it are really the same thing, since as we have seen the good or the end, by which all our actions are judged to be right or wrong, really is what we want. Yielding to temptation is not for him a question of a breach of a law imposed from outside, but it is really sacrificing what we want more for what we want less. How does it come that when we know that something is really what we want more than anything, we yet do something else which will prevent us from attaining this? This is the problem which he considers in the first half of Book VII.

His answer to this question, so far as he gives an answer, may be roughly summed up by the statement that, in these cases, while in a sense we may be said to know that the course we do not adopt is good, we do not really know it in the full sense. And he distinguishes (VII, iii. 5–14) four possible ways in which we may thus know and not know at the same time.

The first case presents no difficulty. We may know a thing, and yet not at the moment use our knowledge. In a particular case we may not think of putting the question to ourselves, Is this action good or bad ? though if we thought of it we should realize at once that it was bad, and that we had really known this all along. He then proceeds to a second possibility. We may know the general rule, that such-and-such a kind of action is wrong, but we may not understand that our particular action is really of that kind. This is the idea expressed by a modern writer[1] when he says: " The special cause of immorality . . . is that indistinctness of conception, which prevents people from seeing under what general head particular actions are to be classed." It is the state of mind of the man who describes with pride how he made a profit of three or four hundred per cent out of a business transaction with the Government, and then goes on, in perfect good faith, to denounce profiteering as unpatriotic and immoral. This describes a real and very important class of cases. His third suggestion is vaguer and of less value. We may have the knowledge, but be so worked upon by our passions that it ceases to mean anything to us, and the statement that this is wrong becomes merely a meaningless collection of words. And his last suggestion also is of no very great value, because it is really only a special case of the first. He says that we may know that actions of this kind are wrong, and that this action is of this kind, but, led away by our feelings, we may let our minds be occupied by another piece of knowledge, namely, that this action is pleasant or desirable.

But of all these suggestions we are forced to make the same criticism. They all describe, more or less well, real states of mind, but none of those described is really the particular one in which we are interested. They none of

[1] J. R. Seeley, *Lectures and Essays*, p. 292.

them describe a condition in which we are really fully conscious all the time that the action is bad, in which we struggle against the temptation, but in which we are finally overcome by it, and do the action, in some way against our own will. And, though in places Aristotle seems to recognize the existence of such a phenomenon, he never really comes face to face with the problem which it raises.

But is this an objection to his general ethical doctrine? It could only be so if his doctrine involved a denial of the possibility of a state of things which we knew to exist, or an explanation of them which was manifestly wrong. But this it does not do. For consider what the real problem is. It is not a question of deciding whether such cases can occur, because it is an obvious fact of experience that they do. But it is a question of giving a correct description of what actually happens in such cases when they do occur. And this is no more of a difficulty for Aristotle than for the advocate of any other ethical theory. For the problem is not a specifically moral one. The conflict can occur equally well when there is no moral question at all involved, when the end which we really want is a purely selfish or even a positively immoral one. It may be a struggle between a selfish political ambition or a desire for wealth, which is really the thing that the man wants most of all, and a sudden overmastering passion which threatens to defeat the attainment of the end. And in many other ways we may in a moment of weakness do an action while all the time knowing, not so much that it is wrong, as that it will inevitably destroy all our own happiness. At any rate, the fact is undeniable, and an accurate description of this fact is desirable equally on any theory. The question at issue between Aristotle and, say, Kant, resolves itself into the question whether the moral struggle is a special case of this, or whether it is something entirely different. And the success or failure of an attempt to give a correct psychological description of the general nature of this struggle does not affect this question.

The other point which deserves a short mention is Aristotle's description of the nature of pleasure, contained in the second part of Book VII, and the first part of Book X. Perhaps the chief interest that we shall find in the account is in considering it as an answer to the question, Does Aristotle's idea of the Good as that which, in some sense, we desire more than anything else, involve the idea that the Good is pleasure or the greatest amount of pleasure ? Or more generally, What view are we to take of the doctrine of Psychological Hedonism, that the only thing that we can desire is pleasure ? We must omit many interesting points of detail in the account and content ourselves with a brief summary of the main points in his description of the nature of pleasure, and its relation to " happiness."

In the first place, for Aristotle pleasure is closely bound up with activity. Activity is the thing which is pleasant. It hardly needs to be said that activity is not confined to actual bodily movements. In fact, these are a small part of it. Any exercise of any of our powers or faculties or capacities, mental or physical, is a form of activity. For instance, one of the most important forms is intellectual activity, the exercise of our cognitive faculties which takes place when we know or think about anything. It is in this wide sense that all pleasant experiences are said to be forms of activity. There are one or two doubtful cases, which Aristotle gives reasons for thinking may be included, but we need not discuss these. The essential point of the theory is that pleasure is always associated with and asserted of a form of activity.

What, then, are the special characteristics or conditions of activity which make it pleasant ? According to Aristotle all human activity is of its nature pleasant. Where pain arises is where we have something getting in the way and hindering its exercise. The activity is then checked and impeded, with a consequent sense of difficulty and strain and effort. A perfect or complete activity would have no difficulty or effort, but would go on free and unimpeded, and if it was directed to any particular end, beyond its own exercise, it would result in the successful attainment of this end. In actual practice, perhaps we never get this absolutely unimpeded and perfect activity. Our bodies and our physical environment get in the way, and check us and produce the feeling of strain and effort and consequent pain. Aristotle thinks that we get nearest to it in certain intellectual activities, in the contemplation of the great eternal truths of philosophy. But in all our human activities we get something of it. The more unimpeded the activity is, the more pleasure there is in it. So that pleasure may be taken as the sign or symptom of this perfection of the activity. We might almost say that it is the consciousness of its being complete or perfect, or, at any rate, the emotional side, what the psychologists would call the "feeling-tone" of that consciousness. The whole account anticipates in a remarkable way the conclusions of some schools of Psychology. One of the leading modern psychologists summarizes his views on the conditions of pleasure and pain in words which express exactly the same idea, when he says : " Whatever conditions further and favour conation in the attainment of its end, yield pleasure. Whatever conditions obstruct conation in the attainment of its end are sources of displeasure."[1]

We may pause for a moment to consider a possible objection to this account, an objection which Aristotle never considers explicitly, but which it is quite easy to meet on his principles. It might be argued that these hindrances to activity are really essential to pleasure. In any particular form of activity the greatest pleasure arises from overcoming difficulties, and the greater the difficulties, the greater the pleasure in overcoming them. But such an argument misconceives the place taken by the difficulties in such an experience. What they do is not by themselves to produce pleasure, but to rouse us to greater activity. It is because there is, so to speak, more activity, because our powers are more completely

[1] Stout, *Manual of Psychology*, p. 245.

brought into play, that there is greater pleasure in overcoming big difficulties than small ones. And of course the pleasure only comes when the difficulty has been overcome and the activity has thus perfected itself.

It follows from this account that pleasures differ, to use Aristotle's phrase, in kind. What this means may be made clearer by an example. Consider, for instance, a colour, say, blue. We call all blue things, blue books, blue birds and the rest, blue, because they have the same colour, they possess a quality in common. And we can distinguish this quality from the other qualities of these objects, their size and shape, for instance, and consider it by itself. We have a distinct idea of it apart from the objects and from the other qualities with which it is found. But now consider another case. Why do we call the different particular colours red, green, blue, etc., colours? On the analogy of the last case, it should be because we find a common quality in them which we call colour or colouredness, and which is the same in them all, so that we can have a clear and distinct idea of it apart from their special characteristics, their redness or blueness or greenness. But we find, if we examine our experience, that this is not so. The relation of colouredness or colour in general to the particular colours is quite different from the relation of the particular colour, say blue, to the particular blue objects. We cannot find anything which we can call just colour apart from any particular colour. We cannot get any clear and distinct idea, or indeed any idea at all, of what colour is which is not any particular colour. In blue, we cannot distinguish the colour or the colouredness from the blueness, for it is not a separable and distinguishable thing. We can only think of colour in general not as a definite quality but as that which takes these different forms. And to assert that pleasures differ in kind is to say that the relation of pleasure in general to particular pleasures or pleasant experiences is analogous to the relation of colour in general to particular colours.

A modern writer has applied these considerations to pleasure. Dr. Bosanquet, in his *Psychology of the Moral Self*, says that if we ask " Is the pleasure in sweetness (or any other experience) a separable element like taste or form or colour so that it can be perceived by itself as a possible object ? " then the answer must be " No." He goes on to argue that if we say that a thing is hot or red, it tells us something about it, what sort of a thing it is or what special kind of thing it belongs to. In his own phrase we convey a perception of a special content. But if we just say that it is pleasant, we do not convey the idea of any definite quality. We have to ask, What kind of pleasantness ? And this is exactly what Aristotle means by saying that pleasures differ in kind.[1]

These considerations enable Aristotle to answer several of the points that had been raised. Thus, as to the question whether we desire pleasure : Aristotle thinks that it is true enough, in a sense, that everybody desires pleasure, just because everyone desires that any activities they undertake should not be impeded but should be exercised freely. But they do not desire pleasure as something by itself, because, as we have seen, pleasures are so closely bound up with activities that they differ in kind, just as activities do, and there is no common element, which we can call pleasure and which we can distinguish from the rest and make our object of desire. Aristotle's own phrases about the relation of pleasure to the activity are that it perfects the activity, and that it is " a super-added end." That is to say, it is the result and sign of the activity being complete, and thus, as it were, puts a crown on our efforts. So that we should not be completely satisfied with our activity unless it resulted in pleasure. But it is not separable from the activity and desired apart from it, still less is the activity desired in any sense as a means of pleasure.

[1] This view of pleasure is not, however, admitted by all modern psychologists. See Titchener, *Text Book of Psychology*, p. 251.

The same considerations apply to the distinction between good and bad pleasures. Aristotle's view is that, in the full sense, some pleasures are bad and some good, just because some activities are bad and some are good. What good and bad mean he has already told us. But here he is concerned to insist that the difference between their goodness and badness is not a difference in the amount of pleasure. If any activity is perfected, it produces pleasure, whether it is good or bad. He would, however, presumably say that, as a matter of fact, what we call bad activities could never be really so free and complete as good ones are capable of becoming, though in a particular case they might actually be more so. This is a further point which does not affect this argument. But it leads us on to a consideration of his final position, to which we must now turn.

The " happiness " which is our final end, must, we remember, consist in the exercise, as continuous as possible, of certain activities. They must be such as are done for their own sakes, not for the sake of any result which they may produce beyond themselves. This is the fundamental Aristotelian distinction between doing and making or action and production. When the point of the activity lies in the exercise of the activity itself, it is doing or action, when it lies in the result which is produced it is making or production. There is probably an element of both in most activities, but the amount varies very greatly in different cases. Thus, the activity of the shoemaker we should probably class as pure production: the point is that the shoes should be made. But even here there is perhaps a small element of value in the actual doing, in the exercise of the faculties involved. As we rise higher in the scale of activities the element of action becomes greater. For instance, in artistic work, in making a statue or painting a picture, the product is itself, no doubt, of value. But the activity involved in producing it is at least of equal value. The joy of creation, the pleasure in the actual work which the artist feels may be greater than the pleasure that is given by the contemplation of his work. We may recall the story of Cézanne, painting his pictures and then destroying them or throwing them away as soon as completed. It is really difficult to say whether the element of action or the element of production is of greater value in such cases.

Now the final end at which we aim must be a form of action. Our final end cannot be simply to produce something, because when it is done, then the end is attained and there is nothing more to do. But where are we to look for this perfect form of activity ? Hitherto Aristotle has spoken of it as if it were to be found in the exercise of the ordinary moral virtues, in what we call doing things, in the active life. Particularly for him is it to be found in the active exercise of the qualities which make a great statesman, and perhaps in a lesser degree in those which make a great soldier, in the courage, energy, self-control, and intellectual grasp which such men must exercise. And never at any time does he doubt that there is absolute value in the exercise of these qualities. But they do not content him as a final account of what constitutes " happiness," and at the end he subjects them to a criticism which attempts to point out where they fall short.

His first and chief point is that these practical activities are never undertaken for themselves alone. They always aim at producing some result beyond themselves. The general exercises his skill, and no doubt gets satisfaction from the exercise of this quality. But he also wants to win the battle ; and if this result is not produced, his satisfaction is not complete. So also the social reformer aims at relieving poverty, and if he fails in this he cannot be satisfied with the exercise of the qualitites which are demanded in his work. In every case the end is, in Aristotle's phrase, not merely the activity but a result beyond the activity. And this element of production seriously weakens the claims of these activities to be considered as sufficient ends in themselves.

In the first place, it means that they do not satisfy us by themselves. At the least, even if we feel that the thing was worth doing, the effort worth making whether successful in producing the result or not, the result produced is at any rate an added satisfaction. In Aristotle's phrase, these activities cannot be by themselves the supreme good, because if they are successful, the result added to them makes them of greater value. In the second place, when part of our object lies in producing something beyond the activity, then, when this result is once produced, a large part of our motive for undertaking the activity ceases. When the soldiers have brought the war to a successful conclusion, then the reason for the exercise of their courage and other military virtues has gone. Of all such activities, therefore, we must say, that they cannot be a complete and final end, because they are never undertaken for themselves alone.

This opens up a larger question, which Aristotle merely suggests. These activities, as we have seen, are directed to producing some result. That is, they are directed towards producing some change in the world as we find it, towards giving it something which it has not yet got or altering or destroying something which is already there. That means that we do not consider the present state of things as being satisfactory: that is why we want to alter it. When we have made it satisfactory, of course, we cease to want to alter it, and any practical activity undertaken then could only make it worse. It is only among the evils of war that the good qualities of the general become active. It is only while people are poor and unhappy that the self-sacrifice and sympathy of the social reformer find their opportunity of exercise. This means, in short, that all these practical moral virtues depend for the occasion of their exercise on the existence of evil, on the fact that the state of things is not as good as it might be and that therefore some alteration is needed. And they are exercised in order to make these alterations and to remove the evil. In other words, these activities are directed towards removing the opportunity for their own exercise. That is to say, they are essentially self-destructive. And further they depend for their possibility on things not being perfect, on the existence of evil. But no one would say that we ought to keep the evil, if we can remove it, in order to exercise these virtues. As Aristotle says, in words which some modern writers might well bear in mind, " We fight in order to make peace." Unlike Bernhardi, he considers that it would be barbarous to make war just for the sake of exercising the military virtues. Or to take our own instance, no one would say that poverty ought to be preserved in order to give social reformers something to do, great as the virtues may be that its existence brings into play. We cannot, therefore, take as our ideal a state of affairs which depends for its possibility on things not being perfect, that is to say, on our ideal not being reached.

This difficulty has attracted the attention of modern thinkers, and some have sought to find in these facts an explanation of the problem of evil. They conceive of evil as existing in order to give human beings the opportunity of exercising the moral virtues in the work of removing it. Thus a modern theologian writes: " Evil is the condition, not the accidental, but the essential condition, of what is in and for itself the best thing in life, namely, moral victory." This view has, indeed, plenty of difficulties of its own. But the point of interest for us is that it is utterly alien to the spirit of Aristotle, as indeed of almost any Greek thinker. A good which demanded as a condition of its existence the existence of some evil would have seemed to him no good at all, a contradiction in terms. And the idea of infinity which it introduces, of evil always being destroyed but always rising up again for us to destroy it afresh, would have seemed to him, if intended as a description of the ultimate ideal, simply abhorrent.

He therefore chooses a different course. The logical conclusion of these difficulties seems to him to be that we should look for our final ideal in some form of activity which is not open to these objections, in some form of activity which is undertaken for itself alone, and does not aim at producing any change or result beyond itself. It must be complete in itself, not self-destructive; and not dependent on the existence of something evil. And he finds this in what he calls contemplation. And probably anyone who wanted to find such a form of activity would have to look for it in somewhat the same direction. The form of it which would probably most readily occur to us would be what we call æsthetic contemplation, the enjoyment of beauty. For there we seem to find an experience, which, within its own limits, fulfils all the conditions of absolute perfection. It does not aim at anything beyond itself, it is not trying to produce any result, it has no element of self-destruction, it is not in its own nature limited in time, and it does not depend on the existence of evil.

Aristotle, however, looks in rather a different direction. The form of contemplation in which he seems to find the necessary conditions of the final end fulfilled is what we may call intellectual contemplation, the contemplation of the ultimate truths about the nature of the universe of which we have gained knowledge. It is not the search after truth, but the truth itself, the complete understanding of the ultimate nature of what is, that is completely satisfying. Even for Aristotle this can only have been an ideal, not completely realizable under the limitations of our human nature. But our own experience gives us glimpses of it. Many of us have now and then felt the keen pleasure that comes from having gained the knowledge of some fact, from having really grasped the nature of something, or from having come upon a big generalization which explains many things hitherto unintelligible. We may sometimes hear a mathematician speak of the beauty of the proof of some proposition, and the pleasure to be got from thinking of it. And the same experience is not unknown to the student of Philosophy. Of course, under actual conditions, we never get this completely, because we never get complete knowledge of everything. And short of this we could not be completely satisfied, because our intellectual apprehension of one point always leads us on to something else and raises fresh questions to solve. But we have enough indication from our own experience to understand the sort of satisfaction that this complete knowledge could give us. And this is for Aristotle the final ideal.

He leaves it in obscurity what the exact relation is between this life of contemplation and the life of practical activity. The latter cannot ever bring complete satisfaction, but it has a positive value of its own. It does not seem that Aristotle regarded the practical life as simply a means of preparing the way for the speculative life, and only of value as doing this. Rather he regards them as co-ordinate forms of the good life, both of value in themselves, but one of much greater value than the other. But what the practical result is he does not definitely tell us. It is uncertain whether he thought that everyone should try to combine the two, or that everyone should try to get rid of the claims of the practical life as far as possible, or—which is perhaps the most probable—that for a few only was it worth while trying to live the life of contemplation while the great majority should be content with the practical life and moral goodness.

The whole idea may be illustrated further by a consideration of the form in which it appears in Christian doctrine. The whole of the great system of Catholic Theology is mainly based on the work of the scholastic philosophers of the thirteenth and fourteenth centuries, who in turn based their philosophy on the work of Aristotle, which they applied with great speculative power to their own problems. The problem of the final ideal presented itself to them in the form of questions about the condition of the souls in Heaven. And in the main they accepted Aristotle's position on this point. The souls in Heaven cannot be thought of as continuously doing something, as making changes in the state of things, because they have reached a condition of perfection. And the only form of activity left to them is the contemplative. It is in the continuous contemplation of the Divine perfection that Heaven consists. And further this perfect bliss in contemplation which the ordinary man can only hope to attain in Heaven is in a far smaller degree open to a few souls on this earth. They find it in living a contemplative life of prayer and meditation, as free as possible from the cares and troubles of the world. Hence the hermits, and the contemplative orders of the monks and nuns. Such a life is the highest possible to man. But only a few are capable of it, and those who have not, in the technical term, the vocation for this life would do wrong in wasting time in trying to attain it.

This introduction of the religious element is not at all alien to the spirit of Aristotle. Indeed, though he does not speak of it in the *Ethics*, we can tell from his other work that he must have meant very much the same thing. He tells us in the *Metaphysics* that God is the ultimate cause of everything that happens in the world: He is the Prime Mover, and is the final cause of everything " as being loved." The contemplation of the ultimate nature or principle of the Universe must, therefore, for Aristotle include, if it does not simply mean, the contemplation of the Divine. And we find his immediate disciple, Eudemus, who wrote a recast in a more popular form of his master's lectures, expressly describing the final end as being " to contemplate and serve God." The Christian God, of course, is not Aristotle's God. But the fundamental identity of thought is remarkable.

With this we must conclude our consideration of Aristotle and his development of the idea of purpose as the fundamental moral fact. We have now to face the task of pronouncing judgment on its value, and considering the objections that have been or might be brought against it.

CHAPTER IX

ARISTOTLE AND THE ETHICS: CRITICISM

WE have now arrived at a general idea of Aristotle's ethical system. Whatever we may say about it, it has at all events avoided the fatal objection which we were able to bring against Kant's system. It at least explains the moral fact in a way which enables us to see why it should be a motive for action. His definition of goodness at least makes it intelligible why the goodness of an action should be taken as a reason for doing it. And that is a great achievement. His definition, at any rate, satisfies one of the main conditions which we laid down for it. And that may suggest to us that there must be at the very least something of value in his doctrine, something that we must retain whatever else we may find it impossible to accept. How much, we have yet to decide. And to enable us to do that we have to consider the objections which have been, or may be brought against Aristotle's position. Some possible objections on minor points we have, indeed, already raised and considered in the course of our exposition. But these were all on questions of detail, and they could all be met by a little further development or a very slight modification of the argument, without in any way departing from Aristotle's main principles. We have now to consider the more serious and fundamental objections which might be brought against the main principles of Aristotle's theory.

We shall probably be justified in assuming that the main line of attack would be against his fundamental idea of the Good as end or purpose, which means the identification in some sense or some form of what we ought to do or what is good to do with what we want to do. And it will be urged that to make this identification really misses the whole point of morality. It is one of our most fundamental moral assumptions that what is good or right is not necessarily the same as what we want. And a view which contradicts this assumption is just as much to be rejected as one which contradicts that other fundamental assumption, against which the Kantian theory clashes. This line of objection may be presented in various forms.

In its extreme form, which would insist upon a complete separation and even incompatibility between what we want to do and what we ought to do, the argument would obviously plunge us straight into the fallacy of Kant, and present us with a moral fact which could never by any possibility be a motive to action for us or indeed of any interest to us at all. So that we begin to see the dangers into which this argument may lead us if not used carefully. One attempt to avoid this particular pitfall might be made by those who would argue that the Good is, indeed, an object of desire and hence a possible motive to action, but that it is a special kind of object of a special desire, different from other desires. Similarly its attainment would give us satisfaction, but a special kind of satisfaction, different from that given by the fulfilment of other desires, and not merely just greater or fuller or more complete than that. But this line of argument, too, has its dangers. For it may easily result in representing the moral impulse or the desire for the Good just as one among many other impulses or desires, differing from them as they differ from each other, but not greater or stronger than they and not including them, in any way. And if we arrive at this point, we shall find it difficult or impossible to show why this particular desire or this particular satisfaction should have any claims over the others or should be treated in any way on a different footing to them.

But finally we may avoid these dangers by another form of this argument. It is true, we may say, that we do really want the Good : it is even true that we do in some sense want it more than anything else, or, at any rate, that it would satisfy us as nothing else could. But, we should argue, that is not the essence of goodness; that is not what makes it good. It is only, strictly speaking, a fact about ourselves that we do in some sense desire what is good. But the goodness of the things which we thus desire does not consist in or depend on this fact. This goodness is a fact about them, a fact of a different kind altogether from this.

But when we have got as far as this, it would seem that the objection has become one of words only. If we assert that it is a necessary fact about the Good that it will satisfy as nothing else can, it is really idle to trouble ourselves about the question whether it does this because it is good or is good because it does this. It is like asking whether a geometrical figure is three-sided because it is triangular or triangular because it is three-sided. They are really two mutually dependent facts about the object, so if we say the Good must necessarily satisfy us in this way, that must mean that it is essentially related to us, that it makes its appeal to us because of a necessary connexion between something in it and something in our nature. Of course, on no theory is that all there is to be said about it, but equally any theory that admits that the Good is necessarily the supreme object of desire, must at least include that in its definition or, at any rate, define it in such a way that that fact about it may be seen to follow from the definition. And if such an important fact about it is a part of or an element in its essential nature, it becomes really a matter of arbitrary choice whether we take that part or another part or both together as our formal definition. At any rate, that fact, if it is a fact, is the thing about it that most concerns us because it is that which gives it a claim on us, which makes it a possible motive to action, which, in short, makes it of any interest to us at all.

But we are still only at the beginning of our objections to the Aristotelian system. Let us admit all that has just been said. Let us agree that the Good is that which in some sense we desire more than anything else. Let us agree, if necessary, to take that fact about it as the formal definition of it, as being the fact about it which most interests us, which gives it its claim on us, or whatever we may like to say. But we are still only at the beginning of the whole subject. We want to know in concrete detail what it is that is thus the supreme object of desire, and hence good. Aristotle has given us his account of this in his account of " happiness," in his doctrine of the Mean, and in his final exaltation of intellectual contemplation as the supreme good. And it is this part of his argument which we may now proceed to criticize.

We should almost certainly object, even on his own assumption, to the inadequacy of his account of contemplation and its objects. He makes it purely an intellectual activity and its objects merely the eternal truths of Philosophy. We have already seen some of the additions which have been or might be made to this. Thus, for instance, the æsthetic form of contemplation of beauty seems to have at least reasonable claims to be put alongside of the intellectual form. And, as we have seen, later speculation, beginning indeed with Aristotle's immediate successors, gave a much more definitely theological turn to the idea. But these are, after all, questions of detail and merely supplement his account by a further application of his own main idea. And there are much more fundamental criticisms to come.

These would probably be directed against the whole idea of " happiness " as the final end. Even allowing for the most extended meaning possible of the word it remains, as we have seen, a state, or if the word " state " gives too much an idea of something passive, let us say a condition of ourselves. What each one really desires is some condition of himself. Aristotle, as we have seen, insists on this, as, for instance, in his criticism of the idea of honour or reputation as the end. But it is just this, it might be argued, that is the fatal weakness of the whole theory.

In the first place, it is not true merely as a psychological fact that we only desire or want some condition of ourselves. In some extreme cases the object which we want may not contain any reference to ourselves at all. We may simply want a state of things to exist or something to happen in which we are not included and which has nothing to do with ourselves at all. We can see cases where men are ready to go to certain death in order to bring about some result, without believing in or thinking about the possibility of their being able to participate in or even to see this result. And there are other cases, more frequent and obvious, where we do, it is true, desire a condition of ourselves, but where we desire it alongside and as part of a condition of other people or other things as well. Thus we may desire the good of our family or our country, where we are thinking, indeed, of ourselves, but only as a small part of a much greater whole. Such cases are too obvious and familiar for their possibility to need argument.

Further—and this is the important point—according to our most deep-rooted moral ideas, it is to these cases above all that we apply the specifically moral predicates, it is these desires and the actions that they lead to which we think of as good or right. Morality, according to our ideas, involves a reference to others beside ourselves. That is the essential element in it, and that is just the element that Aristotle's account fails to appreciate. We may say, in fact, if we are careful of the precise meaning of the words, that morality is something essentially unselfish, while Aristotle's account makes it ultimately selfish.

Something, however, must be said in modification of this criticism. We must not represent Aristotle as consciously setting up a doctrine of selfishness as opposed to a doctrine of unselfishness. Nor need we assert that the practical result of an application of his ideas would be an increase in selfishness. In fact, indeed, Aristotle would probably value unselfish actions as highly as we do. We know that running through his mind all the time is the thought of the statesman whose main concern is the good of others. It is for him indeed that the book is really written : Aristotle was certainly not thinking of his own selfish ends when he wrote it. Further, we know that he thinks of one of the chief forms of " happiness " as consisting in the work of the true statesman whose actions are essentially unselfish and directed towards the good of others. More generally we might say that moral excellence, and hence " happiness," demands the development and exercise of what have been called our " other-regarding " impulses just as much as of our " self-regarding " impulses.

But even if we recognize all this, it will not invalidate the main grounds of the criticism. For, according to the doctrine of the Mean, these " other-regarding " tendencies must not be developed too far at the expense of the others. They are just tendencies in our nature alongside of the others, and they have to be developed harmoniously with them. And the fact remains that, according to Aristotle's own statement, the final end of each man is some condition of himself and it is as that that he desires it. On Aristotle's principles, we should really have to assert this of the statesman as much as of anyone else. We should have to say that in the ultimate analysis it will be found that he really wants to do good to others because in doing this he exercises his own nature, and it is this aspect of it that makes it an object of desire to him. So that however much for the good of others the actual results of his action might be, he does them primarily because he is thinking of and aiming at a condition of himself.

And in his final results, as we have seen, Aristotle destroys the claim of these unselfish activities to be a completely satisfying end in themselves. And he criticizes them precisely on the ground of the existence of this unselfish element in them. For they aim, partly at any rate, at producing results beyond and apart from their own exercise. In acting thus, we are thinking not only of the activities themselves, but also of the results that they will produce and the good that they will do for other people. And it is just because of this fact that he finds them inadequate. So we are presented with the idea of the only completely satisfying end being the life of contemplation, which is purely a condition of ourselves without any element of unselfish activity in it. We seem, then, to be justified in declaring Aristotle's idea of the final end or good to be in this very real sense a selfish one, and thus failing to fulfil one of the first conditions which must be fulfilled by any account of the moral fact before it can be accepted as completely satisfactory.

We pass, now, to quite a different line of criticism, one which is directed not so much against what Aristotle actually says as against what he leaves unsaid, against the inadequacies of his account which will have to be filled in before we can even decide whether it is to be accepted or not.

It is, as we have seen, the primary point in his doctrine that the Good, that is, what we have called the moral fact, is what we want or desire or aim at. " The good," as he says at the beginning, " is that at which everything aims." But it is obvious, and no one is more conscious of this than Aristotle, that not everything that we desire is good. And it is equally obvious that many people on many occasions desire something else which we do not call good more than they desire what is good. And before we can judge and evaluate the doctrine we want much more information than Aristotle gives us about the nature and relations of these frequently conflicting desires, the desire for the Good and the desires for things that we know are not good. In the whole course of our exposition we have been hampered by the inadequacy of the account of the nature of this desire for the Good. We have been constantly reduced to saying that " in some sense " we desire what is good more than anything else. And now we have to face the question seriously which has been hanging over us all the time. In what sense, exactly, can we truly say that we desire the good more than anything else?

A provisional suggestion has already been made as to the kind of answer that Aristotle might have given to such an objection. It was suggested above that all human beings desired the Good in so far as they were human, and that if they did not desire it in any sense they were not really human. And it was further suggested that in a treatise which was primarily intended as a practical guide for the statesman and educator, who would have to deal with men in the mass, such abnormal cases could not be considered. But now that we are trying to get a real account of the facts and to go deeper than would be necessary merely for practical purposes, such an answer would no longer satisfy us. After all, all human beings are human. And there can be no doubt that Aristotle would have said that all human beings really did desire as their end this condition of " happiness " as he describes it. If he had allowed any exceptions, it would have been such beings as are literally abnormal and lacking in something which it is an essential characteristic of human beings to possess, in other words, madmen and defectives. But it is not these cases which trouble us. For it is the ordinary, normal people, whom everyone would allow to be human in any sense, who present us with the problem in its most acute form. It is not on the face of it obvious that for such people to think of a thing as morally good and to desire it are one and the same thing, nor that the more they think of it as good, the more they desire it. We should rather say that the people of whom we could truly assert this were the exceptional and abnormal cases.

Aristotle, of course, sees clearly that people often act from desires which are not good, and he has plenty to say about actions done from passion or emotion, when our particular impulse leads us to act in a way that is positively bad. And in the passage we have already considered he attempts, not perhaps very successfully, to explain what happens in such cases. But even supposing—a rather large assumption—that these cases present no fatal difficulty to his theory, that does not dispose of this criticism. For they are only one side of the matter, these cases where we want something that is not good. The other and more difficult side is where we seem not to want something that is good, where we clearly recognize that some action is good or right, and yet do not desire to do it, or, at any rate, do not desire it strongly enough to do it. We must say, on his theory, that the desire for the good is always there, even in such cases. But how do we know that it is always there? What form does it take? How are we to describe it? We see plenty of cases where people are living and acting in a way which we, and they if the question was put to them, would recognize to be clearly wrong, and yet seem to be perfectly contented in it. And the question that we must ask, is, What is going on in the minds of such people to justify us in saying that they are really desiring the good all the time?

It has been suggested above that the doctrine of the Mean attempts a sort of answer to this question. It represents us as containing in our natures all sorts of instincts and impulses and tendencies to action, so that the most complete satisfaction that we could enjoy would be the satisfaction of all these impulses as far as possible. And we get to this limit of possible satisfaction by developing our natures harmoniously as a whole, so that no one of these tendencies is developed at the expense of the others. But this will not meet our present difficulty. The mere fact of these tendencies being there as potential desires is not a sufficient warrant for asserting that we desire that which is good all the time, even if the good for us is nothing more than the harmonious development of all these tendencies and the greatest possible satisfaction of all these desires. If we merely observe the instincts and impulses which actually exist in people we find that they vary in strength in different people: so that if a particular man had one impulse very strongly developed and another very slightly, to satisfy them both equally would really give him a much smaller total sum of satisfaction than if he satisfied the first at the expense of the other. Further, our impulses grow stronger or weaker according to the life we lead; they can be trained and either developed or weakened. If, therefore, we had nothing to think of but these impulses and their satisfaction, there would be no particular reason why we should try to satisfy them all: it would be just as reasonable to try to weed out some of them or at least to suppress them to a point where we felt no discomfort in satisfying others at their expense.

If the good for us merely meant the harmonious development of all these different tendencies in our nature, we should still have to look for a desire for the good, which was not merely the sum of our particular desires or impulses. We should have to assert not only that we had these particular tendencies and desires and impulses, but also that we had a desire that they should all be developed and satisfied harmoniously without sacrificing any. Such a desire may, of course, be there. But it is not obvious on the face of it. It does not seem that, when by exercising one tendency in our nature we violate another, we always have a conscious feeling of dissatisfaction arising from the frustration of this desire for a complete life. Even if we have, it is clearly not always very strong, or strong enough to influence our actions. And if the good is something more than this, if we desire something else instead of, or as well as this, the problem is even more pressing. We want, in short, a psychological description of this desire for or impulse towards the good and of the forms it actually takes in human experience. We cannot, at this stage, say that it is impossible to give such a description. But we can at least say that Aristotle has not given it.

These, then, are the main criticisms that could be or have been brought against Aristotle's doctrine, these are the main difficulties and inadequacies that we find in his account. We have now to start afresh on their consideration. Some of them we may find to turn out not to be real objections at all. Some we may be able to meet by a further development or a slight modification of Aristotle's ideas. And some we may find to be really valid, so that the theory in so far as it is open to them must be radically altered or abandoned altogether.

PART III

TOWARDS A CONSTRUCTIVE THEORY

CHAPTER X

THE CHARACTERISTICS OF DESIRE

THESE criticisms of Aristotle's account raise several important points, to a consideration of which we must now proceed. And it may be convenient to start with the second class of criticisms, the criticisms, that is to say, which demanded a more exact account of that fact in our natures which we have spoken of, more or less vaguely, as the desire for the good. But before we ask what we mean by the desire for the good, it would be as well to make quite sure that we are clear in our own minds about what we mean by desire in general. We must assume, of course, or rather we must recognize, that we know something about this fact which we are trying to describe. We cannot put ourselves in the position of some one who is trying to describe some absolutely unknown thing by describing the known elements of which it is built up. Further, it is clear that the essential element in it is not something which can be defined or described further or analysed into anything else. But, for all that, there is a good deal to be done in the way of distinguishing this essential element from the surrounding circumstances in which it appears, of describing the conditions of its appearance, and the other elements which it involves.

When we say that we desire a thing or want it or wish for it the essential element in the experience is a certain feeling towards the thing which we cannot define further. By using one or other of these terms in ordinary speech, we sometimes—though not always—imply something further about the character of the objects of the feeling or the probability or improbability of our attaining them. Thus the term " desire " is occasionally used to imply specially the desire for certain physical sensations or experiences, which we are inclined to regard as less worthy or lower objects of the feeling. And " wish " is sometimes used rather specially for this feeling towards objects which we do not expect to be able to attain. But the essential feeling is the same or of the same kind in all cases. And it is with this that we are dealing. We have to try to see what further we can say about this which will be of interest to us in the present investigation. The following points may be suggested :—

1. Desire, as we have seen, is a feeling towards something. It implies, that is to say, an object. We cannot just desire : we desire something. And, in consequence, desire also implies what some psychologists would call an idea ; though, perhaps, for our purposes it would be better to say that it implies some knowledge of what it is that is desired. We need not be detained long over an apparent exception to this, which is suggested by popular use of language. We say sometimes that we " want something, but we don't know what it is." But that merely means that the object of our desire is only very vaguely or partially known to us. It may mean that we know what we want in general, but not in detail. Very often it means that we have a consciousness that things in general are not satisfactory, a vague feeling of discomfort or uneasiness. What we want, in such a case, is to remove this discomfort or uneasiness ; and that is a fairly definite object of desire. But we may have very little or no idea of the reasons for this discomfort or the means for removing it. The statement that desire implies some knowledge of its object does not, of course, mean that we must have complete knowledge of it, a condition which would be rarely, if ever, fulfilled.

2. We have spoken of the " object " of desire, and more ambiguously of the " thing " which we desire or want. And

this is legitimate, if we keep carefully in mind what we mean by it. But, of course, strictly speaking we never desire a "thing" in the sense of a concrete object like a dog or a chair. When we say, as we very often do, that we want a dog, we mean that we want to possess a dog. The object of our desire is, not the dog, but our possession of the dog. In general terms, the object of desire is always, not a thing, but a situation, which we imagine and desire to exist.

3. Closely connected with this is the further point, that desire always refers to the future. In common speech, we say that we only want something that we haven't got. In the stricter terms suggested above, we desire a situation that does not exist or is not a fact. But, while this is undoubtedly true, there is a certain danger of misunderstanding in the application of it. For it might be taken to mean that desire is necessarily for some change in the actual state of affairs. And this would not be true. We might desire that the situation which was actually existing at the moment should continue in the future. We may be enjoying an experience, say the contemplation of a beautiful object, and want to go on doing so. It is true that in such a case the actual desire for the continuance of the experience only arises if we think of the possibility of not continuing. And, of course, in this case as in every other, the desire refers to the future and is therefore not for something present: the continuance of the experience is not yet a fact. But it is important to remember that to say that desire refers to the future is not the same thing as to say that desire is necessarily for something different from the present.

4. We need not repeat the arguments with which we are already familiar which go to prove that desire is not necessarily for pleasure. We may desire a situation to exist, quite without thought of any pleasure or pain to ourselves which is involved in it. More generally, we may desire a situation in which we ourselves do not appear at all, though no doubt we should desire the situation more if it included

our own presence and our own enjoyment of it. We may even desire a situation which will involve pain for ourselves. On the other hand, it is not because the situation is painful to us that we desire it nor is it the particular element in the situation which is painful to us that we desire. If we could imagine the situation, exactly the same in every other respect, but without the element that was painful to us, we should no doubt prefer it. And if we could consider our own pain by itself we should prefer to be without it. But that does not invalidate the truth of the statement that we may desire a whole situation which, as a matter of fact, includes our own pain in it.

5. We have already referred to Aristotle's account of the distinction between a desire for the means and a desire for the end. But, in the light of our present investigation, we may perhaps be able to describe what happens a little more exactly. We should say, naturally, that if an action was only done as a means to an end, we do not desire to do that action, but desire only the end for which it is done. And this is true enough in a sense. If we thought of the doing of that action without thinking of anything else we should not desire it. But, then, why do we do the action? We naturally say, Because we desire the end to which the action is a necessary means. But though this account is not untrue, it does not, perhaps, state clearly enough what happens. In actual fact, it seems rather that the object of our desire is the whole situation, including the attainment of the end and all the steps necessary to attain it. We desire the whole situation, no doubt, because it includes the desired end. But unless the idea which we desire to realize includes the steps up to the end as well as the end itself, the desire remains a mere ineffectual longing and does not issue in action.

6. A point that issues from this is that when we desire a whole situation originally for the sake of some element in it, we may come, by a very common mental process, to transfer our desire to some other element or elements in the situation,

THE CHARACTERISTICS OF DESIRE 121

so that we experience the feeling of desire when we think of these elements by themselves, even though originally we should not have done so. To put it in the language of means and ends, we transfer the desire for the end to what is really only a means to it.

This tendency may have both good and bad results. Sometimes when the means are hard and the end seems very remote, it may help us to keep up our efforts, which otherwise would relax or cease altogether. But it may have the evil result that it makes us hold on to a course, originally started on as a means to a good end, even though it may become apparent that that course is not the right means to the end, and it may make us refuse to reconsider the question whether that course is the right means. It is a frequent phenomenon in political life and work, that some scheme or policy is originally advocated as a means to produce certain results, admitted to be good. And then later the advocates of that policy may come to desire it as something good in itself apart from its results, so that they will not listen to any fresh arguments which tend to throw doubt on the value of its results and merely feel anger towards those who bring them forward. Every one will be able to think of instances of this for himself from among his own political opponents.

We come now to two important points, the relation of desire to purpose, and the relation of desire to our other feelings, the emotions and the sentiments.

7. Purpose necessarily includes desire, but it includes a good deal more besides, and therefore it applies to a much more restricted field of experience. Everything that is an object of purpose is also necessarily an object of desire; but there are many things which are objects of desire which are not objects of purpose.

The difference is partly one of degree. A desire does not become a purpose as long as it remains merely fleeting and momentary: purpose implies a certain degree of permanence and stability in the desire for its object. The term would also suggest that its object was relatively remote and involved some consideration of the means necessary to attain it. It, therefore, includes an intellectual process of reasoning which desire does not necessarily do. But more important is its relation to action. Purpose is, or is expected to be effective, while desire is not necessarily so. Thus we may want or desire several different things, which are incompatible with each other. We may therefore have to forgo the attainment of all these objects except one, without ceasing to desire them. But purpose is only directed towards the object of desire which we do not forgo. If we forgo it, it ceases to be an object of purpose. And we may, therefore, desire or want things which we know to be impossible of attainment, or things the attainment of which does not depend upon ourselves. But if an object becomes an object of purpose, that means that we believe its attainment to be possible, and that we believe that its attainment depends largely, if not entirely, upon our own actions. Therefore, it follows that though we cannot have action without desire, we may and often do, have desires which do not lead to action. But purpose always leads, or is intended to lead to action.

8. Desire is not an emotion or a sentiment. Psychologists are nowadays in substantial agreement as to the feelings to which the term " emotion " should be applied, though there is no such agreement as to the proper definition of it. It is applied to certain particular feelings, differing from each other qualitatively, of which fear and anger may be taken as types. Sentiment is used of a more complex and permanent feeling attitude towards persons or things : love and hate are typical sentiments.

Emotions and sentiments do not share the characteristics of desire noted above. They do not in themselves involve an idea of a situation not yet realized or lead to the passage from the idea to its realization. But they are often the immediate cause of a desire. Anger or love may make us desire to act in a certain way in certain circumstances. This

THE CHARACTERISTICS OF DESIRE 123

must be carefully distinguished from the physical expression which most emotions lead to if unchecked. To take a particularly obvious instance, the emotion of amusement naturally results in the physical action of laughter. But that does not mean that the emotion of amusement could in any sense be described as the desire to laugh. There is no previous idea of ourselves contorting our faces and uttering the sounds which we call laughter, and no impulse to translate this idea into reality. The expression follows immediately on the emotion without any previous thought of it. It is when the expression is in some way or some degree checked, that we begin to think of it and to desire to realize it. There the emotion is the cause of the desire. Similarly, a sentiment may cause us to feel desire towards the idea of a particular situation. The desire, however, is not the sentiment, but one of the possible expressions of it, appropriate to those particular circumstances. The particular situation which we desire varies according to the circumstances, but the sentiment remains the same.

It is frequently maintained that all desire is the result of some emotion or sentiment. But the difficulty about accepting that view arises from the fact that we may desire to feel or not to feel a particular emotion or sentiment. We may even, so to speak, pass the different emotions or sentiments in review before our mind, and decide that we desire some and not others. If all desire is a result of some emotion or sentiment, when we desire to feel or not to feel a particular emotion or sentiment, that desire must arise from some other emotion or sentiment. But it would be difficult to maintain that, at any rate, in all cases. We might hate some one, and desire not to hate them and try to suppress the sentiment of hate. We might imagine what it would be like if we loved them, and desire that state of things. It is difficult to see from what sentiment the desire to get rid of the sentiment of hate could arise. Certainly not, as one could most naturally suppose, from its opposite, from the sentiment which would directly conflict with it, the sentiment of love, because that *ex hypothesi* does not exist in this case. It might be that we desired to feel one emotion rather than another because we found one more pleasurable than another. But even if that were found to be true, it would still be the case that our desire to feel or not to feel this emotion or sentiment was not necessarily the result of some other emotion or sentiment. And, if we adopt the Aristotelian theory of pleasure, it would seem that the fact that some emotions are pleasurable and some the reverse would suggest that their relation to us and our attitude towards them were determined by something more than their relation to other emotions and sentiments.

The importance of these considerations for the investigation of the nature of the desire for the good is obvious. If all desire is the result of a previously felt emotion or sentiment, this particular desire must be the result of a particular emotion or sentiment. But we are then faced by a difficulty to which we have already alluded. For, on this supposition, it is impossible to show why this desire should have any claim to a position of superiority over any other desire, arising from a different emotion or sentiment. There is nothing in any one emotion or sentiment, considered by itself, to give it any superior claim over any other. It is purely a matter of which happens to be the strongest at the particular time in the particular person. Some writers have attempted to take refuge in the idea of some kind of general self-regarding sentiment, which can sit in judgment on the other sentiments and emotions from the point of view of the whole self. But when they come to describe such a sentiment, they find themselves obliged to speak of it in terms so different from those which they use in speaking of any other sentiment, that it really becomes impossible to continue to regard it as a sentiment at all. It appears as something much more like a desire for a particular object, in this case a particular state of oneself.

These considerations suggest that it is impossible to maintain that desire is necessarily the result of a previously felt emotion or sentiment, though it may be in some cases. In general, we must regard it as something more fundamental than the particular emotions or sentiments, and capable of sitting in judgment on them.

9. One other point remains to be dealt with, which will bring us nearer to the core of our subject: and that is the relation between desire and satisfaction. The particular problem, which arises from a consideration of our ordinary ideas and ways of speaking about the subject, may be put in this form:—

We naturally assume that the attainment of our desire is accompanied by satisfaction in us. The assumption requires modification at the outset by the addition of the saving clause, " if we know that our desire is attained." For, as we have seen, in extreme cases the desire may be for the realization of a situation which does not include ourselves at all, as when a man sacrifices his life to save his country without any belief that he will ever see her salvation. But, admitting that qualification, we are all familiar with cases where, as we say, we get what we want and yet don't like it when we've got it. The general statement of the lesson to be drawn from such cases has been expressed by saying that what we want is not always what will satisfy us. The analysis of what happens in these familiar cases may help us to throw light on several of our problems.

Let us consider the classic instance of Rosamund and the Purple Jar.[1] Why, when she had got her purple jar, was

[1] For the advantage of those who are not familiar with this classic of childhood, I append a brief summary of the plot: Rosamund is taken out by her mother to get a pair of new boots. But on the way she is so delighted by the appearance of a large purple jar in a chemist's window, that she begs her mother to get it for her. Her mother explains that she cannot afford to get both the boots and the jar, but the wilful child insists on the jar and declares her readiness to give up the boots. The jar, on being purchased, is emptied of the purple liquid it contained, and turns out to be merely of plain glass. And at a later date Rosamund suffers greatly from not having got the new boots when she could have had them, while her mother does not fail to improve the occasion.

Rosamund still not satisfied, and why did she subsequently regret that she had been given what she wanted? There was really a twofold reason. In the first place, when she had it, the jar turned out to be not purple after all, so that when she consented to give up getting her new boots for the sake of the jar, she was really cheated in her bargain. She did not get what she wanted. She wanted the jar because she thought it was purple, but she did not want it as it really was. Such cases present no particular difficulty.

But there is a further point. We are supposed to assume that, even if the jar really had been purple, yet when she found her boots in holes, she would have wished that she had chosen the new boots instead of the jar. At the time she actually wanted to have the jar although she knew that that would mean giving up the boots. But if she had really understood all that was involved in the choice before her, she would have wanted the boots more, even at the time. We do not need to say that she " really " wanted the boots more all the time. Her actual desire at the time the choice was made was for the jar. But that was only because she did not realize what it would be like to go about with her boots in holes. We may say, if we please, that she had a potential desire for the boots all the time. She, being what she was, would have wanted the boots at the time if she had understood all that was involved in the choice. And, therefore, we may say that if her mother had insisted on giving her the boots instead of the jar, it would not only have been for her " good," in some vague and undefined sense, but it would have been what she would have wanted herself, if she had had full knowledge. Only in that sense can we say that it would have been giving her what she " really " wanted.

Similar considerations apply to objects or situations of which we have had no experience, about which we know nothing or have never thought. We cannot say, in any sense, that the West African natives actually did desire the taste and the effects of gin before the advance of civilization introduced them to it. But we can say that they had a potential desire for it all the time, as was shown by the fact that when they did have experience of it, they desired it very strongly. And the same applies to other and more complicated cases. It means that there is something in the nature of the persons concerned, which is there whether they know it or not, and whether it ever becomes active or not, in virtue of which we can say that they would desire these objects under certain conditions. And the one condition that is necessary to make this element in their nature active, so that they actually would desire these objects, is knowledge, either full knowledge or sufficient knowledge to show us what it would be like to attain these objects of desire.

We are now arriving at a twofold distinction, on the one hand, between mere desire, which may be for any situation which we can imagine, and desire that is to become practical, to develop perhaps into a purpose which can only be for a situation which we believe can be realized. And on the other hand, there is a corresponding distinction between the mere idea of a situation, and the knowledge of the relation of that idea to the reality. We may have a perfectly clear idea, as far as it goes, of a situation which contains elements that could not in reality go together, or which for some other reason could not be realized. Rosamund may have had a perfectly clear idea of a situation in which she had the purple jar, while the holes in her shoes caused her no particular discomfort. But unfortunately for her, reality, including her own nature, was such that the holes in her shoes caused her acute discomfort, so that if she had had a clear idea of the situation which actually occurred, she would not have desired it. In short, full knowledge of the situation means not only a clear idea of the situation as we imagine it, but a knowledge of whether the different elements of the situation which we imagine are consistent with each other and with the rest of reality. Among the elements in the situation, about which we most frequently make mistakes, are our own feelings.

The situation imagined includes ourselves feeling in a certain way, but we need full knowledge to tell us whether we actually should feel in that way in that situation. But that is only one instance of the distinction between the idea of the situation and full knowledge of it. The former is sufficient for us merely to have a desire, but if we are to attain what we desire—so far as we ever can attain it—we must needs have the latter as well.

We have now reached a somewhat clearer idea about the nature and conditions of desire. It has not, indeed, been a complete scientific account of these, but it has perhaps given us the main points which it is necessary to grasp in order to proceed with our special investigation. We must now return to this, and make some attempt to see what light these considerations throw on the question of the Desire for the Good.

CHAPTER XI

THE DESIRE FOR THE GOOD

HOW do these conclusions, if they are true, apply to the particular problem, which we have set ourselves to solve? How do they help us to answer the question, which we wanted to put to Aristotle, about the nature of the desire for the good, or the desire which made what is good, good? It is better perhaps to express it in this last form, to avoid a possible objection, the objection, namely, that by the very fact of speaking or asking questions about the desire for the good, we are implying that goodness itself is something other than being desired, and cannot be defined by reference to desire. But such an objection, we must repeat once more, is only of any force if we totally misunderstand the situation from which we set out on our ethical investigations. As we have already seen, the situation is that we start by knowing or thinking that certain things are good, without any clear understanding of what " good " means. We have already seen reason for thinking that " good " must be explained by, or that it in some way implies, a relation to desire. We now have to return to a consideration of the facts as we know them in our ordinary experience, and to ask whether they are consistent or can be explained consistently with this view. If that is understood, it will be seen that there is no reason why we should not, to begin with, use language which recognizes the distinctions that we make at this unreflective level, even if we are going to rise above these distinctions at a later stage. We may perfectly well, therefore, talk about the desire for the good, without in any way contradicting the idea that " good " may ultimately have to be defined by reference, in some way, to desire.

Bearing that in mind, we proceed to ask what the facts of

experience, which we can observe, tell us about the relation of desire to goodness. Obviously, in the first place, some people at some times do desire things which we call good. Otherwise, of course, no good action would ever be done. Also, it is practically certain, if not quite equally obvious, that we do at times desire the thing which we think good, not because of any incidental advantages, but partly or entirely because we think them good. The presence or the belief in the presence of this fact, which we call goodness, as an element in any situation is sometimes sufficient of itself to arouse the feeling of desire in us. On the other hand, it is equally obvious that being thought good and being desired do not by any means always and necessarily go together. We know too many cases of actions or situations, which we believe to be good or which every one, who really asked themselves the question, would admit to be good, but which are not desired at all by some people. And still more familiar are cases where, though the good thing is desired, it is not desired so strongly as something else, where the desire for the good, that is, does not lead to action. The facts of experience, then, tell us decisively that being good is not the same thing as simply being desired. If it were, there would of course be no problem. But it is obvious that it is not, not only from the facts of experience, but also from the knowledge of the meaning of goodness that we already have. Further than this, however, it is clear that if we look at these facts alone, if we confine ourselves to a consideration of what actual people actually do desire, we shall find no warrant at all for maintaining that goodness has any kind of necessary connexion with desire or that it must be defined by reference to it in any sense.

We shall not, however, get very far in ethical investigation unless we realize that we are not confined to these facts, to the observation of the actual desires of actual people, and further that a consideration of these facts alone will take us a very little way. The illegitimate attempt to confine us within these limits deserves a brief consideration by itself. For purposes of reference we may christen it the Psychological Fallacy in Ethics, because it really rests upon a too exclusive application of the point of view of Psychology to Ethics.

Traditionally, Psychology has taken as its starting point the examination of the " stream of experience." It tends to confine itself, therefore,. to what actually is or has been experienced, to describing, analysing, and classifying this, without asking whether this experience, as we know it, does not point to or suggest something beyond itself. This point of view, perhaps, is perfectly legitimate within the limits of Psychology. But when it is applied to Ethics, it is apt to assume that we ought to be able to find the moral fact in or among these facts of experience, from an inspection of the actual desires, emotions, and feelings which are or have been experienced. It is felt that if morality exists at all, if it is not, as Kant says, merely " a vain notion," it must be reducible to some form or some compound of these. This really amounts to saying that if there is such a thing as morality at all, it must really be something other than morality. And it tries to show how morality is to be derived from experience *minus* morality. A recent writer on Ethics, from this point of view, has asserted this quite clearly. He lays down as the chief problem of moral speculation that of " deriving ethical notions from notions which are not ethical, or of deducing the moral law from the facts of experience and of nature." [G. Pitt-Rivers, *Conscience and Fanaticism*, p. vi.]

But the moral philosopher would absolutely deny the validity of this assumption. He would insist that such an attempt was foredoomed to failure, as surely as the somewhat analogous attempt to deduce the existence of an external world from our own ideas. He would deny, even, that it allowed for all the facts of experience,[2] and he would assert

[1] Even those psychologies which claim to go beyond conscious experience and to deal with unconscious mental processes find themselves describing these in terms of conscious experience, as " desires," " wishes," etc. At any rate they treat them simply as events taking place in the mind.

[2] Because, of course, the moral judgment is a psychological fact of experience just as much as a desire or other feeling. But merely to deal with it descriptively as such does not give us its significance.

that, if we had not got the specifically moral experience to start from, it would be absolutely impossible to deduce it from anything else. He would hold that ethical investigation, if it is ever to get anywhere, must start from its own special data, the facts of morality, of which the chief fact is that we do make moral judgments, that we do recognize a difference between good and bad, right and wrong, and that we mean something by these terms.

The position from which he must start is that we believe that something which we have called the " moral fact," is found in certain things, and is truly predicable of them. To explain what this moral fact is he must begin, not from something else where no idea of the moral fact comes in, but from the knowledge that we have of the moral fact itself. We do not, that is to say, start from a psychological investigation of actual desires or other feelings, from the knowledge we have of them in our conscious experience, but we start from the fact that we make moral judgments, and a consideration of the moral judgments that we do make. We must consider what we know about these, and infer what seems to be the most probable explanation of them. That is not to say that we shall get no help in our investigations from the psychological method. Still less does it mean that at the end we shall be left with the moral fact as something isolated and sharply distinguished from anything else. Obviously our final explanation must show the relation between the facts of morality and the other facts of experience: it may turn out that the relation is very close indeed. But our investigation must start from the facts of morality, and any explanation we give must be tested by the success with which it explains these.

We have seen plenty of reasons why it seemed necessary to explain the moral fact by some kind of reference to desire. But that does not mean that we wish to explain it by a simple reference to actual desire as we know it in experience. We have seen some of the most obvious reasons why this was impossible. And in addition, there is the general consideration that what we desire varies from moment to moment and from person to person, whereas it is one of the most universally recognized features of the moral fact that it does not vary from person to person or from moment to moment. This does not mean a return to the fallacies of Kant, nor the setting-up of universal moral rules, absolutely valid apart from the particular circumstances. But it means, for instance, that for a particular person in a particular situation, a particular action is good or right, even though he does not desire it, or even if, when he thinks of it, he desires it at one moment and not at another. And a particular character is a good one, even though some people might like to be of that character and others might not. In general, if anything is good, it is good whether it is actually desired or not. So that it is clearly impossible to explain goodness by reference to actual desires.

But the case is different if we turn to what we have called potential desire. It is perfectly possible that there are certain objects which, under certain circumstances, would be desired by every one. The fact that they are not actually universally desired would be no disproof of this possibility. In particular, there might be objects which were so related to our natures that, given complete knowledge or understanding of them, they would be desired by every one. Could this be the explanation of the moral fact? Could we say that to call an object good meant that it was an object which every one could not but desire if they realized its true nature?

The outlook in this direction is distinctly more promising. But still we cannot accept such an account quite as it stands, as we shall see if we try to apply it to particular cases. Thus, we say that a certain action or course of action is good or right. If we accepted this account, we should have to say that we meant that anyone who realized what it was like to do that action would desire to do it. But are the actions that we think good always such that anyone who realized what they were like would desire to do them ? The matter could easily be put to the test. There is no better way of realizing what it is like to do a particular action than to do it. And what could we say if we found that some one, having done an action or followed a course of action that we were convinced was right, did not desire ever to do such an action again or to continue following that course of action ?

That this is possible, it would be idle to deny. We may illustrate it from the story of an actual occurrence. A certain workman was an habitual drunkard. He was a skilled craftsman, in spite of his drunkenness which he did not allow to interfere too greatly with his work, and earned high wages. But almost everything he earned went in drink. As far as he was concerned that, perhaps, would not have mattered very greatly. But he had a wife and children, who were always half-starved and in rags, with no furniture in the home. Finally, a lady who was interested in the case, succeeded in persuading him to take the pledge for six months. The effect was extraordinary. He began to save money, the furniture was taken out of pawn, the children were well fed and well clothed, and the wife was happy. However, a few weeks before the end of the six months, the man came to the lady who had persuaded him to take the pledge, and told her frankly that, having now tried both drunkenness and sobriety, he preferred drunkenness. He said that, as he had promised to keep sober for six months, he would keep his promise for the few weeks that remained, but that at the end of the time he had decided to return to his old habits. And this intention he duly carried out.

It is clear, then, that we cannot give this as an explanation of the meaning of goodness in all the uses of the term. Such a case, for instance, makes it obvious that by calling an action good, we cannot mean simply that anyone who has tried it and therefore knows what it is like will desire to do it. But then we know from Aristotle that when we are speaking of particular actions, we call them good in different senses of the word. An action is only good in the full sense if it proceeds from a good character. But, even when this is not so, we may call a similar action good by analogy, as being the sort of action that a good man would do. Thus, in the case we have just described, the action of the man in question was not good in the full sense, because it did not proceed from or express his own nature. He knew, then, what it was like to do these actions, but he did not know what it was like to do them as the result of a formed good character. Because he did not wish to continue the former experience, it does not in the least follow that he would or could have chosen to turn away from the latter, supposing he had gone through it and supposing the choice was open to him.

And there is a further point. We call his course of action during the six months good, even as it was, not only because it was the kind of action that a good man would have done, but also because it produced results on other people which we should call good. It is true that after he had seen these good results, the man deliberately turned his back on them and acted so as to destroy the results which his sobriety had produced. But the essential feature of the good results lay in the state of mind of the wife and children, and to see the outward manifestations of this is not necessarily to know and understand them, to realize what it felt like for his wife and children to be restored to prosperity by his sobriety only to be plunged back into misery again by his relapse. It is still a perfectly tenable position to maintain that if he had realized this, he could not have desired to act as he did.

These considerations may give us the clue we want. And perhaps the following hypothesis will avoid all these difficulties.

Moral judgments, on this hypothesis, imply the notion of an ideal state of things, an ideal situation, which is such that, if it were once known and understood, it would be the supreme object of desire for every human being: no one who realized what it was, could turn away from it or desire anything incompatible with it, or be fully satisfied with anything short of it. That means, looking at the matter from our point of view, that there is something permanently there in the nature of all of us, which makes us so that we should desire this ideal state of things under the condition of full knowledge of its nature. "In the nature of all of us," because it is one of the most fundamental facts about moral judgments as we know them, that if they are valid at all, they are valid for all human beings, perhaps for all conscious beings. Therefore the ideal must have this relation, not to the special characteristics of this or that man, but to the human nature, which we all have in common. It is the fact of this relation to our nature that makes it good, that gives it its claim on us, that makes it a possible motive to action, or, if it were fully known, the strongest possible motive for action. This ideal state of things may never be realizable in its completeness, at least under present conditions. Perhaps, too, it cannot be completely known or imagined by individual human beings. But it is realizable in part here and now, and we can have some idea of what it is like. And in proportion as it is actually realized, and in proportion as the notion of it becomes clearer to us, we desire it more and more.

This is the Good, the supreme moral fact. In making moral judgments about particular things we are really referring them to this ideal, which is implied, even if we do not realize this at the time, in our making moral judgments at all. When we say that a particular thing is good, we mean that it has a certain relation to this ideal. When, for instance, we say that a person's character is good, we mean that it realizes the ideal, so far as it can be realized in a single person's character. When we say that an action is good, we may mean that it proceeds from such a character. Or, again, we may mean that it will help to produce this ideal, is a means to it. But either way it means a reference to the ideal. Perhaps we might confine the term "goodness" to the former of these facts about actions, while if we intended to convey the latter, we should call it a " right " action. But, as a matter of fact, these distinctions between the meanings of different terms like " good," " right," " ought," etc., become of small importance in the light of this view of the moral fact. They are distinctions made at the unreflective level, before we realized what it really meant, and they imply rather differences in the attitude of individual people than differences in the nature of the fact itself. In any case, to assert any moral predicate of any particular thing means asserting a relation to the ideal. To assert goodness of the ideal, means asserting of it this relation to our natures which gives it the power of making us desire it before all else, and of satisfying us as nothing else could.

Many questions remain to be answered before our account can be considered in any way complete. Some must be reserved for more detailed consideration. But one point we may deal with now.

What form does this desire for the ideal take in actual experience ? This is really to ask from what motives people act rightly when they do act rightly. Very few people really grasp the nature of the ideal and desire it accordingly, referring everything else to it. But, on the other hand, there are such things as moral motives in our actual experience, which must be regarded as symptoms or partial expressions of the underlying fact in our nature, which is the potential desire for the ideal, as yet not understood. It is only natural that this should take varied forms in different people and different circumstances.

As a matter of fact, most people have some notion of an ideal, some standard which they are really anxious to live up to. One of the commonest motives which restrains us from doing wrong acts is a dislike of thinking of the sort of person we should be if we did them. We can remember the Gay Lord Quex, who, dissolute *roué* as he was, felt that " there are some things a fellow can't do." Professor Gilbert Murray

[*Rise of the Greek Epic*, p. 80], gives an eloquent description of this state of mind as it is presented in Greek literature under the term Aidos. He speaks of the lawless chieftain who appears free to act just as he likes with no restraints. " And then, as a matter of fact, you find that among his lawlessness there will crop up some possible action which somehow makes him feel uncomfortable. If he has done it, he ' rues ' the deed and is haunted by it. If he has not done it, he refrains from doing it. And this not because anyone forces him, nor yet because any particular result will accrue to him afterwards. But simply because he feels Aidos."

But with this we are really at a lower stage than a conscious reference of the action to some ideal. Aidos is generally mistranslated as Shame. But a far nearer English equivalent would be Conscience. This account really describes very closely that feeling which we call Conscience, that " pain, more or less intense, attendant upon the violation of duty," as Mill describes it. It is a lower stage, because it has not risen to any notion of an ideal to which particular actions may be referred, but considers each action by itself and feels or does not feel thus towards it. But the feeling at this stage is to be taken as an indication or symptom of that underlying fact in our nature, in virtue of which we should desire the ideal before all else, once we had anything like a clear notion of what it was.

Such a result as that which we have arrived at so far is open to attack from two sides. On the one hand, we should be attacked by those who would denounce our whole conception of such an ideal as a mere unproven assumption, and would demand what evidence we could produce for it, what proof we have that we should desire it with full knowledge of it, and so on. But such a criticism really rests on a misunderstanding of the situation. Our task is to find a hypothesis which explains the facts of morality, as we know them. And if our theory does this better than any other, if it describes the moral fact according to the indications that our moral experience gives us of its nature, if it allows for and explains all the glimpses which different people have had of it, then it has received all the proof which we are entitled to demand for it.

We are not called upon to prove it or deduce it from anything else. At the most, we could be asked to show that it was not positively inconsistent with any other established facts. And if any such supposed facts were produced, we should have to consider them. But they have not been produced, and it is difficult to see how they could be. Of course, if our conclusions could be confirmed from a consideration of other facts, we should welcome this additional evidence for them. But the mere lack of such confirmation affords no grounds for objection to the results arrived at from a consideration of the facts of morality as we know them.

Such questions really depend on that deeper difference of principle to which we have already alluded in discussing what we called the psychological fallacy in Ethics. The hypothesis here put forward claims to depend on facts just as much as any "psychological" theory. It bases morality on what it believes to be the facts of human nature. But it denies that these facts are merely those directly revealed in conscious experience. It would, indeed, insist that these facts of experience, if rightly understood, point to something in human nature which is not fully revealed in them, and that only by taking this into account do the facts of experience themselves become really intelligible.

Such is one line of attack which this theory would have to be prepared to meet. The other comes from a diametrically opposite direction, from those who would feel that the account fails to do justice to the unique position of the moral fact by reducing it to mere desire, in whatever form.

Such a feeling, no doubt, in part is mere prejudice. Any description of the moral fact, any attempt to bring it into relation with other facts or to explain it by reference to anything else, must inevitably at first sight, by unveiling the mystery, create a certain sense of disappointment, and detract from that awe with which we are apt to regard things that we imperfectly understand. Particularly, by describing it in terms of desire, might we seem to be lowering its dignity. It would be pointed out that desire is a feeling that we have towards all sorts of objects, worthy and unworthy alike. And even if we refer to a supreme desire, which we should feel under ideal circumstances, yet even so, as long as we make the essential claim of what is good on us a matter of desire in any form, we reduce merely to a difference of degree, the difference between the motives of the noblest and of the basest actions which any human beings commit.

In this last point there is certainly something more serious than mere prejudice. Does the difference between good and bad mean ultimately that we merely desire one more than the other? Is there no such thing as positive evil? These questions have to be seriously considered.

In reply to them, we can only point once more to the difficulties of any alternative view. If our argument has been at all sound, we are forced to define the moral fact in some way by reference to desire, if it is to be a motive for action at all. But there is more than that. The ideal, which is implied in moral judgments, has a positive character of its own : it is not completely described by calling it the supreme object of desire. That is one of its essential characteristics, and it is that which gives it its claim over us and makes it a motive for action. But that is not all there is to say about it. And perhaps prejudices and real difficulties alike will diminish or disappear altogether in face of a completer description of the positive nature of the ideal. It is to the task of giving such a description that we must now address ourselves.

CHAPTER XII

THE NATURE OF THE IDEAL

WE have arrived, then, at the notion of an ideal object of desire, an ideal situation or state of things, by reference to which we pass moral judgments in particular cases. We now have to ask whether we can give an account of what this ideal state of things is: so far we only know that it is what we should desire under ideal circumstances. Aristotle tries to give such an account in his description of what Happiness consists in, and in his final exaltation of the life of contemplation to the position of supreme end. We saw reasons for not being completely satisfied with this account of his. Can we do better for ourselves?

We must first ask how we should set about such an investigation. We have spoken of the ideal state of things as that which would satisfy us completely as nothing else could, if we attained it, or as that which we must desire more than anything else if we really knew what it was. This must mean that it is related to our nature in such a way that it is the supreme object of desire, or, to look at it from the other end, that there is something in our natures that would make us feel like this towards it. We may say, if we like, that it is the supreme expression of our nature. And it might be thought that from an examination of our experience of what we actually do desire or have desired we might arrive at some generalization about the object or objects of human desire which would tell us what the supreme object of desire must be.

But such a hope would certainly be vain. Undoubtedly we can and must get from an examination of desire, as we know it in our own experience, some knowledge of the general nature and the general conditions of desire, which must hold of any possible cases of anything which can be called desire at all. Something of this kind has been attempted in the preceding chapters. And such knowledge is essential to us in our present investigation. But that is a very different thing from drawing conclusions about the ideal object of desire from the actual objects of the actual desires of ourselves or other human beings under the limiting conditions of the present life. To believe that from a knowledge of what we actually do desire it is possible to deduce what we should desire under ideal circumstances is to assume a much greater direct knowledge of our own natures than we actually possess: any one person is always much more than is shown in any particular set of circumstances. We recognize this in everyday speech when we say that we never know how a person will act in sudden emergencies or unexpected circumstances. And it is even more impossible to infer from what we do desire in the circumstances in which we live to what we should desire under ideal circumstances of perfect knowledge and enlightenment, to which we can never attain completely but only approximate more or less.

We shall have to turn elsewhere for the evidence on which we can base our description of the ideal. We must remember that the belief in an ideal object of desire at all was not derived, and could not be derived, simply from our experience of our actual desires. That, indeed, showed us that the belief was not inconsistent with the rest of our knowledge, and, of course, without experience of particular desires we could not even form a notion of an ideal object of desire. But, of itself, it gave us no grounds for positively asserting the truth of this notion. We could hardly, then, expect that it would give us much, or any, guidance in describing the positive nature of this ideal object of desire. And, just as our belief in the reality of such an ideal was based on the fact of our moral judgments, so it is to these that we must look for any information that we can get about its nature. They express, in the metaphor that we have already used, the glimpses that

THE NATURE OF THE IDEAL 143

we have had of the moral fact. And it is from these glimpses that we may hope to be able to build up some account of its nature.

At the outset, we come face to face with one cardinal fact which our moral judgments tell us about our ideal object of desire which could not possibly have been inferred from an examination of our experience of particular desires. This latter by itself would give us no reason why the supreme object of desire might not be different for each individual, or why the attainment of this supreme object of desire by one individual should not be incompatible with its attainment by another. But our moral judgments tell a very different story. It is one of the most certain glimpses that they give us of the moral fact that the ultimate ideal must be the same for all, that the final good for one man cannot possibly clash with the final good for another. And the account which best allows for this evidence is to say that the ideal is not merely some state or condition of ourselves, but that it is a general situation which includes others besides ourselves, and that this, in the right circumstances, would be equally desired by everybody.

The next point that we notice in an examination of the general characteristics of moral judgments is that they always refer finally to conscious, living beings. And the conclusion to be drawn from that is that the ideal must be a situation of such beings. We could not, for instance, conceive of the ideal object of desire as being a condition of inorganic matter. Further, it would probably be agreed that we must accept Aristotle's demonstration that the ideal must consist in some form of activity of these conscious beings, using the term " activity " in its widest sense. And, adding the results so far attained together, we arrive at the notion of what we may call a social ideal, that is, of a community of conscious beings, in a certain condition of activity and related to each other in a certain way.

Our notion of the ideal is getting clearer, but it is still far from precise. Another step forward will be taken in considering Aristotle's argument for the superiority of action to production where he tries to show that the activity in which we must believe the ideal to consist cannot be an activity undertaken for the sake of producing a change in the state of things that we find around us. His argument certainly seems of great weight, so far as it goes. But, on the other hand, we find that our moral judgments attach great importance, perhaps the highest importance, to some of those activities which seem to be undertaken primarily for the sake of producing some result. And this makes it difficult for us to accept his final sharp separation between the practical and the contemplative activities, and his preference for the latter. The problem for us is to reconcile the two points of view, and to do this we have to look for some form of conscious activity which will share the characteristics of contemplation that make it a claimant to the position of supreme end, while at the same time maintaining a much closer connexion with all those practical activities to which the majority of our moral judgments apply. Knowledge or intellectual contemplation, as described by Aristotle, does not fulfil these conditions, because it has no necessary connexion with these practical activities. If we could conceive a community of conscious beings related to each other by perfect knowledge, one of the other, we could see that there would, so far as this relation went, be no place or reason in such a community for any of these practical activities. We have, therefore, to look elsewhere.

We find the nearest approach to the object of our search in some form of the sentiment of Love.[1] This itself, as Aristotle at times seems to see,[2] is a form of contemplative activity. It is complete and perfect in its own nature, and is not made more so by any action to which it may lead

[1] In its active exercise, of course, not as a mere disposition to love.
[2] I believe that the germ of the whole view here developed is to be found in Aristotle's account of friendship in Books VIII and IX. But the treatment there is, undoubtedly, very obscure and confused.

in particular circumstances. We may value the action to which it leads in such circumstances, we may, for instance, be glad of an opportunity to sacrifice ourselves for those we love, because this is to us a test or a proof of the strength of the sentiment in us. But even if there is no occasion for such action, the sentiment remains the same. On the other hand, love does lead, as we have seen, to practical activity in appropriate circumstances. For instance, if those we love are in pain or danger or any unsatisfactory situation, our love for them leads us to action in order to change their situation for the better. But our love for them remains the same, whatever their situation, and, of course, we should not wish them to be in an unsatisfactory situation, in order to give us an opportunity of action that will improve it. Here, then, we seem to have the kind of activity which is similar to the contemplative activity in those points which Aristotle laid down as necessary conditions for the supreme end, while at the same time it is directly connected with the practical activities which form the subject of our moral judgments.

This view enables us to see the position of the practical activities in their true perspective. They owe their value, when they are more than a mere means to the attainment of the ideal, to their being the appropriate expression in the special circumstances of the sentiment of love. If the love did not express itself in those actions in those circumstances, it would not be perfect. But the love remains the only thing good in itself in all circumstances. No particular form of practical activity and no particular set of circumstances is necessary to it, once it has attained to perfection. In particular, this view resolves the problem which we have spoken of under the name of the paradox of self-sacrifice. We know that ordinary moral thinking regards self-sacrifice as among the highest goods. On the other hand, reflection makes it difficult to accept it as an end in itself, because it presents us with a picture of a state of things in which each individual is trying to sacrifice himself, while no one of them is willing to accept the sacrifice of the others. But on our view, it becomes clear that self-sacrifice is of such great value because it is the expression and the sign or proof of supreme love in the circumstances which make it necessary. On the other hand, the circumstances which make it necessary do not increase the perfection of the love or add anything to it: we cannot regard it as an essential element in the ideal that there should be such circumstances present as would make acts of self-sacrifice by some one necessary.

These considerations also help us to understand how we are to regard the ideal. In more primitive stages of thought it has been thought of as a concrete state of things which we may at least hope to realize at a definite point of time. And so we get the different ideas of Heaven with which different religions have presented us. Our description of the ideal, so far as we have gone at present, would then be envisaged in the form of a heaven consisting in a community of souls whose sole activity lay in loving one another. It is not for us to decide here whether there are any grounds for our looking forward at some point of time to the actual realization of such a state. The exercise of imagining it, whether it is ever to be actual or not, may help some minds to grasp more clearly what we mean by the ideal, because it presents them with a picture of the elements of absolute value in our life isolated, in imagination at least, from the elements whose value is only derivative. But what must be insisted on here is that it is not necessary to our view to assume that the ideal is thus actually realizable. And we must certainly not think of it as something which is only realizable at all at some time in the future. It is that element in our conscious life which is of absolute value, which we should desire for itself alone if we had full knowledge of what it was, and its importance for us in no way depends on the possibility of its actual existence apart from the other elements.

The ideal situation, then, which is the supreme object of

THE NATURE OF THE IDEAL

desire is, so far as we have gone, the relationship of love between conscious beings. That is what is of final value for itself in any situation, and the other elements in a situation can only be judged according to their relation to this. The relation of these other circumstances to the ideal will, of course, vary. They may be circumstances which will help or hinder the attainment of the ideal, which will tend to increase or intensify the love that exists, or to hinder its growth. Such circumstances help to bring into existence the sentiment of love in actual cases, but they do not add to its value: if the sentiment was produced without those circumstances, its value would be precisely the same. Similarly with the circumstances which call on those who feel the sentiment to act in a particular way, as when those we love are in a situation in which they need our help. Such circumstances do not add to the value of the love we feel, which would be the same whether they were there or not. Of course, in any conditions of life that we know of there are always circumstances which call on us to express the love that we feel by one kind of action or another. But these circumstances and the kind of action that they call for vary from time to time and from person to person, while the love remains the same : its value does not depend upon its being called on to express itself in this action or that. On the other hand, it is clear that, if the circumstances called on our love to express itself in a particular course of action, while other circumstances hindered or prevented the action —as might happen if one we loved needed our help while we were lying ill or at a great distance from them—we could not rest satisfied with the existence of our feeling of love which was unable to express itself in the way required. In that sense, the other circumstances may be described as forming an element in the ideal situation. But it is only a negative requirement : the circumstances must not be such that they call for a particular kind of action and at the same time prevent our taking it. And, of course, the importance of the circumstances depends entirely upon their relation to the sentiment of love, which is the element of permanent and absolute value.

Is there anything further in the ideal situation beyond conscious beings related by the sentiment of love to one another? Is there any other form of conscious experience which is of absolute value in itself? In particular, what are we to say about Aristotle's candidate for the position of supreme end, intellectual contemplation or knowledge? It is clear that some form of knowledge or cognitive activity is involved in the ideal situation even as we have described it. We cannot feel the sentiment of love towards another being without in some way or some degree being aware of that being. A certain degree of knowledge or intellectual contemplation is therefore involved in our description of the ideal situation, and that not merely as a means to its realization but as an essential part of it. But we can probably go further, and say that perfect love in itself implies and demands perfect knowledge and understanding. For without that we should be loving those that we loved not as they really were but as we thought that they were: and this, surely, could not be thought of as completely satisfactory. So that, if this argument is sound, we may add to our account of the ideal situation, and say that it consists of conscious beings related not only by the feeling of love, but also by perfect knowledge of one another.

The case is rather different when we ask whether the ideal situation must include not only perfect knowledge of the other conscious beings whom we love, but also knowledge of other things as well. Is, for instance, knowledge of the physical universe a good in itself? Many thinkers would maintain that perfect knowledge can only be of the whole, and that, therefore, perfect knowledge of other conscious beings would necessarily involve perfect knowledge of everything else as well. Whether this is so or not is a metaphysical question which could only be decided after a prolonged consideration of many problems altogether outside of our present subject. The doctrine in question certainly does not follow from an examination of our moral judgments nor from our experience of the sentiment of love. And our general ethical position does not depend upon its truth or falsity. It would, however, enable us to pronounce judgment in our particular problem. And as it would be impossible here to undertake the necessary metaphysical investigations, we must be content to leave this particular question in doubt, as the moral judgments of mankind do not seem to pronounce with any certainty on it. We cannot, then, say definitely whether knowledge, other than the knowledge of conscious beings, is a necessary part of the ideal situation. But this uncertainty of ours is less serious in practice than might be thought, because such knowledge is certainly of the greatest value as a means. When we consider the possible circumstances which might hinder our acting in the particular way which our love would lead us to do, we shall find that ignorance is one of the greatest and commonest of these hindrances. And anything that removes this ignorance is, therefore, so much to the good.

Is there anything else that has any claim to be considered as an element, in its own right, in the final ideal? What, for instance, are we to say about the position of pleasure? Of course, we are not going to repeat the elementary errors of Hedonism, and separate the activity in which the ideal situation consists from the pleasurableness of that activity, and then ask whether the activity is not more desirable with the addition of pleasure. The ideal activity is, as we know from Aristotle, in its very nature pleasurable, just in so far as it is complete and unimpeded. But there are other pleasant experiences and forms of activity, and the question is whether the addition of these would not make the ideal situation, as so far described, even more to be desired than it would be without them. What, we may ask in particular, is the relation of the various forms of bodily pleasure to the ideal? Of course, within our experience we often find that the pursuit and enjoyment of certain bodily pleasures may be positively incompatible with the pursuit and realization of the ideal as described. And in such a case the verdict of our moral judgments is unmistakable: the bodily pleasure must be sacrificed without doubt or hesitation. But this is not always the case. And the question is whether the ideal situation of conscious beings in a relation of love and knowledge to each other with the addition of some form of bodily pleasure or something analogous to it would not be desired more than would such a situation by itself.

No doubt, any pleasurable experience is, in itself, desirable. And it might therefore be reasonably thought that the addition of any pleasurable experience would make any other pleasurable experience more desirable. But it is very doubtful, as a matter of psychological fact, whether this is so, and whether the argument does not rest on an illegitimate application of the idea of measurable quantity to pleasure. If we think of an experience as completely pleasurable as it is possible to be, and then try to imagine a different pleasurable experience added to it and going on at the same time, it is very doubtful whether we should think of the result as more pleasurable, or whether, so far as the pleasure went, we should desire it more than the single experience. And, if we should not, it follows that we have no reason to demand the addition of any other pleasure to the activity which we have described as the ideal, and which, so far as it is complete, is completely pleasurable.

The situation is a little different with regard to pain. Not only is it clear that the addition of a painful experience of any kind would make us desire a situation less, but it is also generally recognized in ordinary moral judgments that the diminution of human pain is in itself a highly moral object of action. Of course, as Aristotle points out, pain of any kind, as a general rule, tends to hinder and impede our activities. So far it is to be regarded as evil because

THE NATURE OF THE IDEAL 151

of the hindrance it opposes to the realization of the ideal. But there is more than this, because if we imagined a situation (which is, at least, imaginable) in which the ideal activities, as we have described them, were going on unchecked but accompanied by some form of pain, we should certainly not regard such a situation as completely satisfactory. And therefore we may fairly say that the absence of pain is a negative condition of the ideal situation, not only the absence of the pain which arises from the obstruction of the ideal activities, but the absence of any kind of pain at all.

We have now arrived at a much more definite notion of what the ideal situation is, and of what forms of conscious experience are good in themselves. Everything else on which we pass moral judgments at all is judged by its relation to this ideal. Particular actions are to be judged as they tend to produce this ideal situation, or as they tend to remove the external circumstances which are incompatible with it, or as they express in particular circumstances the state of mind in which the ideal situation consists. Characters of individual human beings are to be judged as they realize in themselves this ideal situation. Many problems remain to be cleared up, and much greater detail could no doubt be attained than is possible within the limits of this work or indeed of any single work. But we shall get some further insight into the matter if we try to apply the results so far reached to some of the most familiar problems of ethical speculation. It is to this that we must now turn.

NOTE

ON THE SENTIMENT OF LOVE

To avoid breaking the thread of the argument, I have deferred till the end of this chapter a discussion on a criticism which might possibly be raised. It might be objected that I have assigned to love such a prominent place in the ideal situation without anywhere attempting a definition or explanation of what I mean by the term. Love, it might be argued, is a term used in many different senses, and applied to things as different as sexual desire on the one hand, and on the other a general kind of enthusiasm for humanity in the abstract, which is quite compatible with an active dislike of particular human beings. It is not, therefore, justifiable to make such prominent use of the notion of Love without explaining in what sense the term is used.

I recognize the justice of this criticism up to a point. I do not admit that I am bound to give a complete picture in concrete detail of the ideal character. But it is certainly desirable that something should be said about the different forms of the sentiment of love, and the moral significance of the fact that the sentiment does take these different forms, to all of which we apply the same name. The position, in my view, is this: Both an examination of the particular forms which the sentiment takes in our experience and the evidence of our moral judgments point us to the idea of a complete or ideal love, of which there are many one-sided and incomplete manifestations in human experience. From each of these incomplete manifestations we can learn something about perfect love: but we err if we take any one of them as complete and sufficient in itself. And we must use the evidence of our moral judgments also: it is not enough to examine the different forms of love, as we see them around us, and try to extract a common element from these. In ordinary speech we tend to apply the term "love" to any sentiment or state of mind in which there is present the simple feeling which the psychologists call "tender emotion." But this feeling is present in the most varied states of mind. It is compatible alike with the attitude of mind which leads to the most devoted forgetfulness of self, and with the attitude that is always making exacting demands on the object of the emotion. It can exist side by side with the most clear-sighted understanding and with the traditional blindness of the lover. We cannot, therefore, take it as the only essential

THE NATURE OF THE IDEAL

element in the love which is part of our ideal, though undoubtedly it is one essential element.

Or again, sometimes we find in family affection and more especially the love of parents for their children, an almost perfect type of the highest form of love, as far as it goes. But if the feeling stops short at the family, and turns, as it sometimes may, into indifference or dislike towards those outside the family, then it is so far imperfect. Of course, though, we must recognize that with limited human beings there must be different degrees of love for different people. It is an imperfect world, and there are some people in it whom it would be very difficult to love. But, apart from that, we must recognize that our capacity for love is limited by the limitations of our knowledge. Love, in the full sense, is only possible for those people with whom we are personally acquainted. It is only in a watered-down form that it can be extended, even by the best of us, to the whole of humanity. We can desire the welfare of the whole of humanity, and that is an essential element in perfect love. But we cannot be said to love them in the full sense. It is always a practical problem how to adjust the claims of our immediate surroundings with those of humanity as a whole. But it presents no theoretical difficulty to our doctrine. The personal ideal for each man may be represented by the notion of a focus of love on those we know personally extending, in this gradually modified form, to the margin of the whole of humanity. [1]

Perfect love, then, includes the "tender emotion" and the desire for the welfare of those loved. It is an attitude of mind which expresses itself in certain kinds of action and in certain emotions in appropriate circumstances. But to describe this further, it would be necessary to describe all the different circumstances in which it may express itself differently. In our own experience we may find partial and limited examples of it, such as those suggested above, which enable us to understand to a certain extent what it would be like in its perfect form. And the Christian will, of course,

[2] We may note here that our doctrine gives us negative information which is perfectly clear and definite, as, for instance, that the feeling of hatred is always and necessarily bad.

hold that we can see it in this perfect form in the person of Christ.

CHAPTER XIII

REASON AND FEELING

A SUBJECT of controversy which has been very prominent in writings on Moral Philosophy is the question whether moral judgments, or morality in general, should be considered a matter of reason or a matter of feeling. In one form or another, this dispute has appeared in most modern ethical investigation, and it has been at times declared to be the great dividing line between different schools of moral theory. It is not very easy to formulate briefly the different arguments for the opposing views, because no two writers have presented their views on this subject in exactly the same form: in particular, it is often difficult to reconcile the account of either view given by its opponents with that given by its supporters. But, in order to illustrate the standpoint that the view outlined above would have to take towards these questions, we must attempt to state very summarily some at any rate of the arguments that have been brought forward on either side.[1]

The advocates of the claims of reason are chiefly concerned to urge that a moral judgment is not simply a statement that the person who judges feels in a certain way towards

[1] Partly for the reasons just stated, and partly because I wish to discuss certain subjects rather than the views of particular thinkers, I have not quoted in this connexion the statements of any one writer. I have collected contributions from several different quarters, and presented the whole in my own language. Most of the arguments which I have given may be found, sometimes in a slightly different form and always with much added, in the works of modern authors. The student may refer, in particular, for the " case for feeling " to many passages in Dr. Macdougall's *Social Psychology*, and to the first few chapters of Prof. Westermarck's *Origin and Development of the Moral Ideas*, and for the " case for Reason " to the ethical writings of Dean Rashdall, in particular his little book, *Is Conscience an Emotion?* But it must be clearly understood that these writers are not to be held responsible for the form in which the different points of view are stated in the text.

the action or whatever it is about which he is judging. To assert that it was, it is urged, would be to deny any moral fact at all. If there is such a thing as goodness or rightness at all, it must be a fact which is there, which is present in some things and not in others, whether we like it or not or, in fact, however we feel about it. For that is implied in our very notion of the moral fact. And further it must be present where it is present, whether we know it or not. So that we must assume that there is a possibility of being right or wrong in our moral judgments. If one man judges an action to be good, and another judges the same action to be evil, the judgment of the one must be true and that of the other must be false. It is implied in our making a moral judgment that, if our judgment is true, the contrary judgment must be false. This is true of moral judgments just as much as of any other sort of judgment. And that means that the rightness or wrongness of an action is something there to be discovered, and not something which depends upon and varies with the feelings of the particular person at the particular time. Any particular action is right or wrong, whatever we or anyone else may think or feel about it. To say otherwise is to deny that there is such a thing as morality at all.

Further, one form of the opposing view argues that moral judgments are simply the result of certain feelings which we have towards the object about which we judge, a specific emotion which we may call the emotion of approval or disapproval, or some other feeling. But, it is urged, this is only half the truth, if that. For it is equally true that the feeling of approval or disapproval is the result of the judgment. We only have the feeling of approval towards an action because we judge it to be right, and because we think that it would be right, even if we personally did not happen to have this special feeling towards it. A quality that varied with our particular feelings would not arouse this emotion in us. And if, by the intellectual process of reasoning and thinking about the action and its nature, we changed our opinion about it and arrived at the conclusion that it was not right, then the feeling would be changed, too.

These are some of the chief considerations put forward on the one side. But there are weighty arguments in favour of the claims of feeling.

Perhaps the chief argument is that which we have already considered at some length. That is, that the moral fact, whatever it is, must be a motive to action. And a mere intellectual judgment, the mere cognition of the nature of anything could not possibly move us to action. Reason alone is not a possible motive to action. Conscious action is only taken as the result of some feeling: all that reason can do is to show us the right means to doing what our feeling impels us to do. So that, if moral judgments are to lead to action at all, they must be ultimately a matter of feeling.

Further, it is urged, in the argument already mentioned, that, whatever may be true in later developments, in the first place it is some feeling towards the object of judgment that leads us to make the moral judgment about it at all. The feeling is there, and without it we should never come to make moral judgments. It is sometimes even argued that there is no reason to suppose that there is anything there but the feeling. The tendency to erect our feeling about a thing to the dignity of an objective fact about it is merely a primitive tendency which further enlightenment will show to be baseless, like the child who says, " But it's nice ! " to a person whose tastes differ from his and who does not like something that he likes.

There are other arguments which have been or may be used. And, of course, besides this there is no doubt a certain prejudice in favour of feeling. It is felt vaguely that feeling is something definite which is certainly there, something that we can be quite sure about, and that to base moral judgments on feeling is to give them a certain basis in undeniable fact. But, leaving this aside, the arguments already given are perhaps those whose consideration will best illustrate our own point of view.

For the point of view which we have so far adopted would really in the main accept both these lines of argument, so far as they go. But it would differ from both positions, in so far as they held that these two lines of argument were mutually exclusive. For this would seem to hold that it is a question between two alternative views only : on the one hand, the view that the moral fact was simply an objective fact, there whether we knew it or not and whether we liked it or not, to be recognized by reason alone ; and on the other, the view that the moral fact was simply the actual existence of a certain feeling or feelings towards certain objects, and that the moral judgment simply consisted in the statement that we, who judged, felt like this towards that which we judged about. But our view would hold that these two alternatives do not exhaust the possibilities, and so it would be unable to accept either of the opposing views in their complete form.

Thus to the advocates of the claims of reason, our view would say, " It is true that the moral judgment is a real judgment. That is to say, it is arrived at by a cognitive process, and it asserts the presence of certain facts which are there whether we recognize them or not, so that our judgment about them may be wrong or right. It is certainly not a bare statement that we feel in a certain way towards a certain thing. But that is not all that there is to say about it. We must go further, and ask what it is that this kind of judgment deals with. What sort of fact does it assert to be present or not present ? It is a judgment about the moral fact, and one thing that we can be sure of about the moral fact is, to repeat our old argument, that it is something which can be a possible motive to action. And to be a possible motive to action it must be or include some sort of feeling. So that, while the moral judgment is no doubt a real judgment, an intellectual process, it must finally refer to some feeling.

"But that does not mean that it refers to some feeling, which we or some other individual is actually feeling at the moment. It refers rather to a potential or hypothetical feeling which we, and we must assume everyone else, would feel in the appropriate circumstances. To be more particular, on our theory to judge that an action is good or right is to judge that it has a certain relation to the ideal which we should desire more than anything else if we had complete knowledge of what it was. But this is certainly to assert an objective fact about it, in the sense that it asserts something about the action and its relations, which is there to be discovered, and about which we may be right or wrong, something, that is, which is there or not there in fact, whatever we or anyone else may think about it or feel about it."

To the advocates of the claims of feeling we should speak in a somewhat similar way. We should say, "It is true that to be a possible motive for action, the moral fact must be or include some relation to feeling, and the moral judgment must finally refer to feeling of some kind. But that is quite different from saying that it asserts or refers to the actual presence of some feeling in us here and now. We could illustrate the difference by an instance which would be recognized as of common occurrence by anyone. When we judge that a certain action is the best means to an end which we desire, our judgment refers ultimately to feeling and it is because it does so that such a judgment could be said to be a possible motive for action. But it is none the less a real judgment for that, a cognitive process of reasoning, which may be right or wrong, because it asserts a fact which is or is not a fact independently of this judgment. And it certainly does not necessarily mean that we have a particular feeling towards that particular action, considered by itself.

"Again, with regard to the assertion that the actual presence of a particular feeling is always the ground of a moral judgment. This may or may not be true, as a matter of fact. It is certainly very often the case, and it seems probable that we should not begin to make moral judgments in the first place without such a feeling. But even if it were always true, that would not mean that there was nothing there but the feeling, or that the judgment was nothing but an assertion that we felt in a certain way at the moment of making it. What it would mean, on our theory, is that we had the feeling, and then took that as a sign or proof that the action or object towards which we had the feeling was good or bad, quite independently of our having the feeling towards it. The feeling would be the ground of the judgment. But if we asserted that there was in actual fact nothing there but the feeling, this would mean that the feeling could not be taken as the sign of the presence of anything else, and that therefore we were not justified in taking it as the ground of our judgment, or, in other words, that every moral judgment was necessarily false. To say that there was nothing in the judgment itself except the feeling, that we did not assert or think that there was anything there except our own feeling, is the same thing as to assert that we did not and do not make moral judgments at all. And that would be to fly in the face of manifest facts."

This last point raises some questions of interest, which call for further consideration. We must recognize that, even if the account does not apply universally, it is at any rate very often the case that a moral judgment consists in inferring, from the existence of certain feelings in our consciousness, certain facts about the object—whether it is an action or a character or anything else on which we can pass moral judgments—towards which we experience that feeling. And the question inevitably suggests itself, How does it come about that, from a mere feeling in ourselves, we infer the existence of some fact outside ourselves, independent of our knowledge of it and independent of the feeling that we have?

If we were conducting a psychological inquiry, in which

REASON AND FEELING

we were confining ourselves to conscious experience or at any rate to what went on in the mind, we should probably have to content ourselves with registering the fact that we do thus pass from the feeling to the judgment. At most, we could say that it was a general tendency of our natures to do so, that we were just made like that. If we did arrive at any further explanation, it would still be in terms of something that happened in the mind. But if that were the only explanation of any kind possible, it would be obvious that there would be no reason to suppose that the judgment was true, in fact there would be every probability that it was false. And when we came to realize that that was the only reason why we came to make such a judgment, we could not rationally go on believing that it was true.

But, as we have already seen, our inquiry is not of this kind, and we must not forget that that is not the only reason which can be given why we arrive at a particular opinion. If we judge that A is B, we may explain this by saying that there is a tendency in our nature to judge that A is B, or that certain things happened in our minds which forced us to make this judgment. But there is always the possibility that there may be another reason which could be given why we made the judgment that A is B: and that is, that A really is B. The two kinds of explanation are not, of course, incompatible. But we have to be clear that the purely psychological explanation is an incomplete presentation of the whole fact, and that by itself it gives us no information about the truth or falsehood of the judgment. If we assert, in any particular case, that the psychological explanation is the only one that can or need be given, we are really asserting that the judgment in question is false (though, even then, it might well be doubted whether the psychological account by itself gave a complete account of the real situation).

And so we see that, in the special case of the moral judgment, the dispute, if there is a dispute, is not necessarily about what actually goes on in the mind in the process of making such a judgment, but about whether the judgment is false or true. We may or may not agree that we judge that a certain action is good because we have a certain feeling towards it. But if we do agree, the further question arises whether this is a valid ground for the judgment. We may put the question more in detail thus :—Is the fact that we have such a feeling towards anything a proof that that which arouses the feeling is good, and would be good just as much even if we did not have this particular feeling towards it ? Or, if not an infallible proof, is it a good reason for judging that it is probably so ?

To answer such a question satisfactorily we must remember what it is that we are judging about, and what it is that we are asserting about it. If we were judging that an external object, of a different kind to ourselves, had certain qualities or was of a certain nature, it is difficult to see how we could say that the fact that we had a certain feeling towards it was any kind of ground for our judging one way or another. The chemist who is trying to discover the nature and properties of some element does not examine his own emotions in order to guide him in his search. But the subject-matter of a moral judgment is not like that. We are judging about the actions or the characters of ourselves and of human beings like ourselves. And we are not asserting about them that they are of a certain nature or have certain properties in themselves, but that they bear, directly or indirectly, a certain relation to our own natures, or to the universal human nature which is the same in all of us. More especially, we are asserting of them that they are so related to our nature that they would be an element in that which we desired before all else, if we had full knowledge and understanding. And such being the case, it is not unreasonable to take a certain feeling of ours towards such objects as a sign or an indication that what calls it forth is so related to our nature. The special emotion is, as we have already described

REASON AND FEELING

it, the symptom of the underlying desire for the ideal, which expresses itself thus in those particular circumstances.

But, after all, we ought not really to speak of the emotion of approval or whatever we are to call the feeling or feelings on which we base moral judgments, as a simple feeling on a level with the other feelings. As Butler says, the special moral feelings, whatever we call them, claim an authority, a special position which other feelings do not possess. And that is equivalent to saying that, if we are to call them moral at all, they are something more than mere feelings. For if they were merely this, we could not speak of them thus. A simple feeling in itself cannot be said to " claim " anything : it is just there. But what we have called the moral feeling is not merely a simple feeling : it is rather a complex attitude of mind which contains much more than the mere feeling. The argument given above in our summary of the case of the advocates of the claims of reason is undoubtedly sound. In the moral attitude the feeling depends upon the judgment just as much as the judgment depends upon the feeling. More generally we may say that the feeling or emotion which is present in the attitude that we call moral approval implies by its presence that we are thinking about the object of the emotion in a special kind of way, that we are putting ourselves at a special point of view : and the feeling arises in us when and because we are looking at the object from that special point of view. Thus, if we are considering any situation and we ask ourselves, Do I like this ? we are considering the situation by itself in reference only to the immediate effect on ourselves and the feeling which it arouses in us. But if we ask ourselves, Do I approve of this ? we are considering it in relation to our whole self, and in the light of a permanent rule of life. We are asking ourselves whether it conforms to a supreme principle of action, to which all other principles of action must give way, if necessary. And it is only if we put ourselves at this point of view that we experience the particular feeling which is an element in the attitude of moral approval or disapproval.

It is important to remember that, if our view is correct, the special quality of feeling that we find in the attitude of approval or disapproval is not the only feeling in the moral point of view. In the highest stage of moral development this particular feeling takes a comparatively unimportant place. It corresponds rather to that stage in the development of our moral ideas to which we have already referred, when we are conscious of the presence of the moral fact in certain cases, but have no clear idea of what sort of thing it is. It is a higher stage when a man has reached a more or less clear vision of an ideal, the realization of which he desires before anything else, so that he identifies himself with it and judges everything by it. At such a stage of development the distinction between liking and approving, between " I ought " and " I want," sinks into the background or disappears altogether, because the man wants the realization of the ideal and whatever will lead up to it, or because the man has so far realized the ideal state of mind in himself that the actions to which it would lead are those that he desires to do. At such a stage the special feeling of approval or disapproval plays a very small part : as far as the man's own actions go, at any rate, there would be no need for it and he would cease to feel it at all. And at such a stage of development, the moral judgment, the intellectual element in the moral attitude, would also change its character. It would no longer consist in taking the presence of a particular feeling as the ground of a moral judgment about a thing. It would start from the ideal whose nature had been clearly realized, and it would consist in exploring the relation of the object of judgment to the ideal situation, in seeing whether it was a means to its realization or what place it occupied in it. That is the highest stage of moral enlightenment.

But, at any stage, the intellectual work to be done in applying the moral point of view includes much more than merely making a judgment on the ground of a certain feeling. Whatever we are judging about, whether it is a particular action, a general course of action, an individual character, or anything else, there is always a great deal of work to be done in discovering what the true nature of the object of our judgment is. For the object is never a simple thing, which we know completely at once. It is always complex, and there is always a great deal about it which it is difficult to discover. Before we can ask whether an action is right or a character good, we must find out with some degree of certainty what that action or that character is. And that, of course, is just the difficulty. There is always the possibility that we may not be seeing the object of our judgment as it really is. We only know a part of it, and we have to infer a great deal about it. And there is always a danger that, even in considering what we do know, we may not attend to all the elements in it in due proportion, but may look too fixedly at one side of it and ignore the rest.

It is clear, therefore, that even when we do feel the emotion of approval towards anything, we cannot judge with absolute certainty that it is right or good, though it gives us a certain probability. We have considered this particular feeling as an expression or symptom of the underlying fact in our nature which would make us desire the ideal state of things if we clearly understood what it was. And we take the presence of this feeling in particular cases as an indication that what arouses it has a certain relation to this ideal. But it is always possible that the feeling may have been aroused by something which we know imperfectly and which we believe to be other than it really is. In such a case, the feeling may be aroused by what we wrongly think to be there in the situation, and not by what really is there. That is one possibility: and there are others.

The feeling may be aroused by some association which that which arouses it has for us, of which we may not be clearly conscious. Or it may be, and very frequently is, aroused in us by suggestion from others. We all know how much our moral ideas depend upon what we have been taught, upon custom and habit, upon what we find other people doing and thinking. There are those who have been so struck by the extent of this that they have argued that all morality was nothing but a matter of custom, habit and imitation. But this is obviously a very superficial view. Obviously, the fact that our ideas of what particular things are right and good are affected by habit and imitation does not in any way warrant us in saying that morality is merely a matter of custom. If the two were the same, it would be difficult to see how we could explain the obvious fact that we do make a distinction between the two, that we think we are saying different things when we say that anything is right or good and when we say that it is customary or habitual. And it would be absolutely impossible to see how we could ever come to criticize a custom or habit on moral grounds, or how there could be any change or development in moral ideas and moral practice. Customary ideas about morality no doubt are important and have a very strong influence: but they could not arise in the first place, and they could not have such an influence, unless there was somewhere what we may call first-hand moral experience for them to work on.

These considerations help us to see how people come to have different opinions in particular cases about what is right and what is wrong, and how it is that moral ideas change from age to age. But, if the opinions are really different, it is a necessary assumption of moral thinking that one is right and the other is wrong. And, as a matter of fact, the difference that there is, is generally greatly exaggerated. After all, the different opinions, especially the opinions of different ages, are generally arrived at in different circumstances, and the difference of circumstances does affect the rightness or wrongness of an action. A course of action may be right in one set of circumstances and wrong

REASON AND FEELING

in another. In such cases, the error, if error there were, would consist, not in holding that the one course of action was right in the one set of circumstances and that a different course of action would be wrong in those circumstances, but in holding that the one course of action, because it is right in those circumstances, must therefore necessarily be right in any other circumstances. Nearly every one would admit, for instance, that it may be right for a government to act in a great crisis or emergency in a way in which it would be absolutely wrong for it to act in normal times. And the same may apply to the different circumstances of different ages or different stages of civilization. And the real error that we commit in forgetting this consists, as we shall see more in detail later, in assuming that it is possible to repeat exactly the same action in entirely different circumstances, whereas in reality it becomes a different action.

This discussion has taken us considerably beyond the immediate subject of this chapter, which was to apply the results we had arrived at to the old dispute between the claims of reason and of feeling. But it has certainly helped us to get a clearer idea of some points in the application of our theory. We may seek further clearness by a very brief application of it to some other problems and disputes which have arisen in the course of ethical speculation.

CHAPTER XIV

SOME MINOR PROBLEMS

WE may proceed further to test and illustrate our conclusions by applying them to various ethical problems which have been raised at different times. These points must here be treated in a rather cursory and disconnected fashion, and we cannot expect to do much more than merely touch on the main conditions of the problem.

1. The question has often been raised in ethical discussion whether, in passing a moral judgment on an action, we judge it by its motive or its results. It will be remembered, for instance, that Mill, in his *Utilitarianism*, commits himself to the assertion that the motive has nothing to do with the morality of an action.[1] It is to be judged entirely by its results, that is, by whether it produces a balance of pleasure or of pain.

To a very superficial view, our account might seem to lend a certain amount of support to this position. In cases where we approve of an action because we think that it is the right means to the realization of the ideal, we seem to be judging it by its results quite independently of the motives from which it was done. But even if we keep on this ground and judge of the action by its results alone, we shall see that we cannot thus neglect the motive from which it was done. For, from the moral point of view, one of the most important results to be considered is the effect that the action has on the character of the agent. And this effect depends much less on the external characteristics of the action than on the spirit in which it is done. So that even if we looked at the results alone, we could not ignore the motive.

[1] " Though," he adds, " much with the worth of the agent." This extraordinary opposition of the goodness of the action to the goodness of the agent raises even greater difficulties which we need not discuss here.

But our view would go deeper than this and deny the legitimacy of the abstractions on which the above argument is based. If we try to think what the action is, apart from the motive, we shall find nothing with any positive character of its own except the mere external movements. And these by themselves cannot be the subject of a moral judgment at all. The subject of the moral judgment proper is the external action as expressing a certain state of mind. The real action, at any rate from the moral point of view, includes the motive. And it includes more than that, if we are to take motive in the narrower sense in which it tends to be used in ordinary speech, which restricts it to the desire or feeling element in the total state of mind which leads to the action. The total state of mind is more than the feeling element. The ideal involves perfect knowledge as well as perfect love. And an action taken in the spirit of love may be, through ignorance or stupidity on the part of the agent, an ill-advised action from the very point of view of the end which the agent set before himself. As such, the action falls short of the ideal, and so far must be condemned. It merits the condemnation that we imply in the use of the term, " well-meaning."

It will help to clearness of thought on this question if we grasp the distinction between passing a judgment on an action already done by ourselves or some one else, and passing a judgment on the practical question what we ought to do in any particular case. In the former case, the above considerations apply. But when we are asking, with a view to action not yet taken, what is the right thing to do, the situation is different. Here we no longer have to think about motives, because it is not open to us to choose from what motive we shall do an action. The motive is already given us, we assume it and do not have to think about it.[1] But we do have to think very carefully about the probable results

[1] There are certain minor qualifications to this (as, for instance, that we must be clear to ourselves that we are not deceiving ourselves about our motives) which do not affect the main point and need not detain us here.

of our action. It is possibly because Mill failed to make this distinction with sufficient clearness that he fell into the way of speaking which we have quoted and criticized.

2. From the general position that has been outlined it becomes possible to reconsider the resolution of the contradiction in ordinary moral thinking which we noted at the beginning of our investigation, the contradiction, that is, between the idea that there is more merit in doing what is right when it is unpleasant, and the idea that the highest development of morality is to like doing right. Obviously, on our theory, there can be no doubt which of these two views represents the truth. It is clear that the highest development of morality is, to use the rather inexact phraseology of popular speech, to like doing right. But that does not dispose of the question, because, if we are true to our principles, we are bound to make some attempt to show how it is that ordinary moral thinking so often comes to the belief that there is some special moral value in doing right when we do not " like " it. Perhaps the process of thought that leads to this idea will become clearer by the examination of an imaginary instance.

Suppose that I have an invalid friend who is ordered away for his health. Suppose that I, having no other claims on me for the moment, at his desire go away with him to look after him and to bear him company. Such an action would be generally admitted to be good, and on our theory the goodness of the action consists in the affection for my friend which leads me to take the action. But, quite apart from my affection for my friend, I may enjoy travelling and like the place he is going to. Or, on the other hand, I may dislike it intensely so that I should never have gone there, except for his sake. Would the action be of a higher moral value in the latter case than in the former? If the strength of my affection for my friend is the same on either supposition, then we can only say that the moral value of the action is exactly the same in the two cases. But it is not difficult to see why we come to suppose that it differs. For it is obvious that such an action taken in spite of an intense dislike of the place is a much stronger and more certain proof of the strength of my affection for my friend than it would be if I liked doing it on other grounds. In the latter case, so far as anyone else could judge, and even sometimes so far as I myself could judge, my affection for my friend might not be strong enough to induce me to go with him, unless I wanted to do so on other grounds. And if this were the case, of course the action would be of less moral value or of no value at all. But on the other alternative, we can be sure of the strength of the affection. The disagreeable attendant circumstances do not increase the moral value of the action. But they afford a convincing test or proof of the strength of the affection which gives it its value.

Of course, what we very often mean by saying that there is no merit in an action that we like doing, is that an action which would be good if done for what we may call moral motives, would not be good if it were done because we wanted to do it for other reasons. And this is perfectly true. But then, as we have already seen, from the moral point of view, it would not be the same action.

3. Somewhat similar considerations apply to the other problem of ordinary thought to which we have referred, the importance of external circumstances and environment from the moral point of view. Here again there can be little doubt about the results of the application of our view to this problem. We should say that there is no question that characters of individual people are, at the very least, affected by their external circumstances. And our view compels us to say that in judging people's characters, we have to judge them as they are, and not as they were or might have been under different circumstances. The relation of a particular character to the ideal is a fact which we have to discover. And it is such a fact that we assert in any particular moral judgment. But we shall find many prejudices in favour of a different view. It would be said that it would "not be

fair" to condemn a man for things which "he couldn't help," which were the result of external circumstances over which he had no control, that we must make allowances for a man who has "never had a chance," and so on. It is easy to refute such a view. We can point out that we have to judge the whole man as he actually is, and that the abstraction of what he is in himself from what he is as a result of external circumstances, which such a view would demand, is an impossible and, indeed, a meaningless process. But it is more important to discover how such a view could come to be held, what are the assumptions at the back of it, and what is the truth which it contains.

The view recognizes the truth that, in judging actions or character on the evidence of actions, we cannot judge simply by their external form, but must take the circumstances into account and allow for them. Thus, for instance, of two men, A may commit a theft under great temptation, while B does not steal, never having had any temptation to do so. It does not follow necessarily from this that B is a better man than A. He may have even less objection to stealing in itself than A, and merely have refrained from doing so because he always had enough money to satisfy all his wants. A may have had a great struggle before he yielded to temptation, while B may be of such a character that, if he had been exposed to temptation, he would not have resisted at all. Then B is definitely a worse man than A. But, on the other hand, supposing that B, thanks to favourable surroundings and to not being exposed to temptation at critical moments, develops a formed good character, so that he would resist temptation even if it came to him, while A, after a long struggle against the temptations to which his circumstances expose him, at last gives way, and gradually deteriorates utterly in character, then B is definitely a better man than A, whatever they were to begin with. We may say that it is not "A's fault," that he has "never had a chance," and we may pity him for this. But that will not make him other than he is.

The confusion is easier if we think, as some people are apt to do at times, of moral judgments as the sentences of a judge passed on a series of actions, and resulting in the apportionment of rewards and punishments, extrinsic to the actions themselves or to the results on the character which they produce. If Heaven is a reward of this kind, then considerations like these might be in place. But if Heaven is a state of mind, then if you are not in that state, you are not, and it makes no difference whether you once were or whether you would have been if the circumstances had been different.

4. Another question which is a " standing dish " to ethical investigation is the question whether there is such a thing as an indifferent or neutral action, an action which is neither good nor bad, to which moral judgments do not apply at all. And here common sense and ordinary modes of speech answer decisively in the affirmative : it is the speculations of ethical thinkers which have led to the possibility of such actions being doubted or desired. It is clear how such a denial would follow from certain views, as for instance, the Utilitarian view, that the goodness of an action meant that it produced a balance of pleasure over pain, and that the badness of an action meant that it produced a balance of pain over pleasure. Every action has some effect in the way of producing either pain or pleasure, and therefore every action is either good or bad, or at least—for it is perhaps just conceivable that there might be an action which produced an exactly equal amount of pleasure and pain—it is always possible and legitimate to ask this question about every action, and to apply this criticism to it.

Our principles, for once, bid us take the side of common sense rather than that of reflective thinking. It is probably true that common sense unduly limits the application of moral judgments and thinks of certain things as purely indifferent which a more exact investigation would reveal as proper subjects for a judgment of right and wrong. But on the main question, whether all actions must necessarily be judged as right or wrong, our view will agree with common sense in giving a negative answer.

On our view, as we have seen, a good action is an action which proceeds from and expresses enlightened love. But that does not mean that an action which proceeds from any other motive is necessarily bad. An action is only bad if it is incompatible with the expression of love, or if it proceeds from a state of mind which is incompatible with the existence of the sentiment of love. Some states of mind, as for instance, the sentiment of hate, are obviously incompatible with the sentiment of love (towards the same person or persons is, of course, understood). But there are others which are perfectly compatible with it, though not essential to it. And these states of mind, and the actions which proceed from them, are, in themselves, neither good nor bad. So far as they do not affect the development and expression of enlightened love in us, they are morally indifferent. If I smoke, because I am fond of smoking, so long as it does not affect anyone else, the action is perfectly indifferent from the moral point of view. But, of course, it becomes bad if I let my fondness for smoking lead me to smoke when it is annoying or injurious to other people, or when it decreases my own efficiency or hinders my work. Apart from this, however, it is difficult to see how we can possibly say that the fondness for smoking, and the actions that this leads to, are either bad or good.

On the other side, it might be urged that any act, however innocent it may appear, may have some effect which will help or hinder the attainment of the ideal, or whatever we make the end of moral action. And, therefore, every action should be considered and judged in the light of the moral principle. But this conclusion would really only be warranted if we could maintain not only that every action may, but that every action must, have an effect in helping or hindering the attainment of the moral end. And on our description of the nature of the moral end, it is difficult to see how this could be maintained, except in the sense in which it would be maintained as a metaphysical doctrine that ultimately everything is connected with everything else. But it is impossible to take this point of view in practice. There are an endless number of actions, which so far as we or anyone else can see, either in considering them beforehand or after they have been done, will have or have had no effect one way or the other on the attainment of the ideal as we have described it. And if we cannot possibly see any effect of this kind, we cannot make such actions the subject-matter of moral judgments, nor can we decide in practice whether to do them or not by moral considerations. In such cases, the action cannot be said to express a state of mind which could be called either bad or good.

The discussion is of value if it makes us recognize that there is always an obligation on us to make sure, as far as it is humanly possible, that there are no moral considerations at stake before we decide some practical question on other grounds, grounds of our own pleasure or what not. We are always taking a certain risk in leaving moral considerations out of account in any particular case: and if we find that our action has a bad effect, which we could have foreseen, then we are blameworthy, even though it was not the effect which we intended. But it is a risk which we do take, and in practice must take on countless occasions: for we should never act at all, if we were too meticulously scrupulous about every action, and on the majority of occasions the risk is justified.

5. A consideration of our view will also enable us to appreciate the truth that lies in the statement that "a man ought to act according to his conscience," or that "if a man thinks that an action is right, it is right for him," and to reconcile this with the belief that there is an absolute standard of good and bad, and that if an action is right, it is right whatever we or anyone else may think about it. Perhaps the important distinction between the point of view of the

man who is passing judgment on an act already done, and the point of view of the man who is asking himself what is the right thing for him to do, here and now, will help us here also.

From the one point of view the statement is really a truism. If we want to do what is right, then all that we can do is to think out what course of action is right, and then, when we have decided according to the best of our judgment, to act accordingly. But, if we are wise, we shall not fail to bear in mind the possibility that we may be mistaken, and that our course of action, instead of producing the good results that were intended, may produce bad results which we should deplore. In such a case, the fact that we thought that it would produce good results will not alter the fact that it actually did produce bad results, and was therefore the wrong thing to do..

From the point of view of judging the action afterwards, the case is rather different. It is no longer a question of asking whether this or that is the right thing to do, but of what place in the scale of moral actions we are to assign to the action already done, how nearly or remotely it approximates to the ideal standard. In the case just considered, assuming that the action was inspired by the highest motives, that it was done in the spirit of the purest love and most single-hearted desire to realize the ideal, then so far it expresses the ideal state of mind. But if it was also the result of avoidable ignorance, of stupidity or lack of enlightenment, and if it was because of that that it failed to fulfil its intentions, then the action was so far bad, definitely worse than it would have been if its motives combined love and enlightenment. What is meant by saying that, even in such a case, the person " ought " not to have acted otherwise, is that, if he had acted differently, even if he had done the action which would have produced the good results he desired, *from another motive*, particularly from an unworthy motive, then he would have shown himself a worse man than he did in his mistaken but well-meaning action. And this is quite true in the case imagined, because we have imagined a man who is actuated by the highest possible motive, and who is quite clear about the nature of the moral standard and only in error about its application to a particular case.

But there are other possibilities, which would alter the situation. For instance, if we suppose a man with a generally strong feeling that he ought to do right, but no clear idea of what rightness means or consists in. Suppose he has formulated a moral code for himself on the basis of some passages of the Old Testament, and believes in righteous cruelty and vengeance and visiting the sins of the fathers upon the children, and suppose in addition he has absorbed a Puritan creed of the sinfulness of all pleasure and enjoyment. Suppose in some particular case he is convinced that his duty bids him inflict some great cruelty on another person, but that his natural kindliness asserts itself, and he yields to temptation, as he regards it, and shows mercy. Surely, in such a case, from every point of view we should say that the man did better to act against his conscience than with it. The value of an act depends on the spirit in which it is done, and an unenlightened and unintelligent " sense of duty," without understanding, does not rank very high among possible motives of action.

6. The next, and last, problem which we may attempt to consider in the light of our general point of view, is the moral relation of means to ends. Does the end justify the means ? Is it right to do evil that good may come ? It is tempting to answer simply, what is obviously true as far as it goes, that of course the end justifies the means : if we will the end, we will the means to it. As for doing evil that good may come, it is really a meaningless phrase : because if good comes of it, and it was done with that intention, it cannot be evil. But the matter is not quite so simple as that, and it will be as well to distinguish carefully.

As we have seen, the goodness of an action does not depend on its results but on the state of mind which it expresses.

It is conceivable, then, that a good action may have bad results. Or, if we assert that the bad results may generally be taken as an indication that there was something wrong with the state of mind that resulted in the action, at least, it will be admitted without question that a bad action may have good results, which were not foreseen or intended. But even if the good results more than counterbalance the bad, that will not make the action anything else but bad, a sign and expression of an evil state of mind. That is one sense in which it is true to say that the end does not justify the means.

From the point of view of practical decision, the end does always justify the means, in the sense that the course of action which will produce a balance of good results in the circumstances should be the one adopted. But there is a certain danger in the application of this principle which makes it intelligible why some have looked askance at it. We cannot say without further qualification that, if the end set before ourselves is good, any means that may help to attain it is also good and therefore to be adopted. For the particular course of action which may be the best means to this particular end, may also produce other results which are not desirable: and if, on striking a balance we find that this course of action will produce more evil than good, it should, of course, not be adopted. We must not isolate one particular end or result, and judge of the means to that, without considering all the other results that the adoption of these means will produce.

These are only some of the problems to which we might apply our principles. But, such as they are, they will suffice to illustrate the method of their application, and the results we get by it. And in the process we have certainly arrived at some increase of clearness about these matters. One point, in particular, on which we have seen fresh light is the importance of the distinction to be made between the two different points of view from which moral judgments may be passed on actions: the point of view from which we try to pass judgment on the moral value of an act already done, and the point of view from which we ask ourselves the practical question, What is the right thing to do in these circumstances? In the one case, we try to judge what state of mind the action indicates, and judge that according to the closeness with which it approximates to the ideal. In the other case, we assume the state of mind and have to ask ourselves what results the action will produce, considered in all its bearings, and then to decide whether these results are those which we are aiming at. To the practical question, asked from the latter point of view, there is, in any given case, only one right answer: that is to say, in any set of circumstances, there is one course of action, and one course alone, that the perfect man, the man inspired by complete love and knowledge, would follow. So far, then, every action is either right or wrong. But that does not mean to say that, in judging of actions which have been already done, from the former point of view, we can divide them by a sharp distinction into good and bad actions. On the contrary, we have, as it were, to assign them a place on the scale of goodness: and the place may vary infinitely in different cases. It would, perhaps, be convenient and in accordance more or less with ordinary usage, to distinguish the judgments passed on actions from these two different points of view by the use of the terms " right " and " good " respectively.

But we must be careful not to exaggerate the difference between the two points of view. They both depend on the same reference to the ideal, and they cannot arrive at contradictory results. An action cannot be " right " but not " good." Why we sometimes speak by analogy as if it could be, is because a man may, from unworthy motives, do an action the external features of which resemble the kind of action that would be done by a perfectly good man in the same circumstances But that does not really mean that the action is right. The distinction between right and wrong in this sense does not apply to it at all, because the distinction itself assumes the good motive, and can only be made when we start from that assumption. Rightness in this sense, is an abstraction from goodness. The judgment about goodness has a wider field, and may take a judgment about rightness, and the action that such a judgment leads to, as part of its subject-matter.

Such are some of the results to which these investigations lead. And further investigation of this kind might lead to further results. But that work must be left to each man who accepts our general principles, to do for himself. We must turn to a bigger and more general subject, the consideration of the relation of Ethics to other branches of knowledge. We have already said a good deal in the course of the discussion about the relations of Ethics to Psychology. We now are faced with the question of the relation of Ethics to Metaphysics.

CHAPTER XV

ETHICS AND METAPHYSICS

MORALITY, as we have so far described it, is based on our human nature. It implies, that is to say, an ideal, which has a claim on us because it is related to our human nature, or because it expresses our human nature, if we like the phrase, in such a way that, with complete knowledge of it, we should desire it before all else. The necessary assumption of our view of the moral fact is that we are of such a nature that we should thus desire the ideal if we had knowledge of it.

But further than this we are not warranted in going from an inspection of the facts of morality alone. Our view, which we believe to be provable from such an inspection, is consistent with many different views on other and wider questions, such as the questions, which are the peculiar subject of Metaphysics, about the general nature of reality and the place of human nature in the whole Universe. We cannot say that our view depends upon any particular view on these questions, or that it could, by itself, be taken as decisive evidence for or against any such view. On the other hand, a consideration of it inevitably suggests further questions, which can only be answered by a prolonged metaphysical investigation. This cannot be attempted here: we can only indicate some of the further questions which arise and some of the possible answers that may be given to them.

On the basis of our present results we must say that the claim which the ideal has on us depends on our being of a certain nature, namely, of such a nature that we should desire it supremely if we had complete knowledge of it. The ideal situation, which has this claim on us, is of a certain character because human nature is of a certain character.

That is all we can say with any certainty from an examination of the facts of human morality. But is it all that can be said at all? Is the moral fact based on nothing but the facts of human nature? As we know, human beings, or indeed conscious life of any kind, have only been in existence for a very short period of the earth's history; and it is probable or certain that in time to come they will disappear again. Assuming that they did not continue to exist on any other planet, does that mean that the difference between good and bad, or right and wrong, will disappear with them? Does the difference depend upon the actual existence of beings such as ourselves? If there were no conscious beings at all, or beings of an entirely different nature from us, would moral judgments cease altogether, or become of such a different nature that they had nothing in common with ours?

The question of what the situation will be when there are no beings like us in existence at all, is not, of course, of very great practical interest to us now. And we do find hints in our ordinary moral speech and thought which suggest that we believe this to be the case, that with the disappearance of beings like us moral distinctions would also disappear. Thus, for instance, we find that we do not pass moral judgments on the actions and characters of lower orders of being, of animals, for instance, or inanimate objects. On the other hand, we find that we do pass moral judgments of a kind on different stages in natural development. We say that men represent a higher stage than animals or inanimate objects, and we mean more by this than simply a later stage. And we feel that if men disappeared altogether it would be definitely a retrograde step.

This may, of course, be merely an illegitimate extension of moral categories beyond the limits of human life. And, even if it were, that would not affect the validity of moral judgments and moral distinctions for human beings. On the other hand, on certain assumptions, this extension may be perfectly legitimate. It would be perfectly legitimate, if

ETHICS AND METAPHYSICS

we held that morality was based not merely on human nature, but on the whole structure of reality, that the moral processes which went on in and for us were in some way a reflection or expression of some sort of analogous process going on in the universe as a whole. If this were so, it would, no doubt, strengthen and confirm our view. But if it were not so there would be no reason to doubt or abandon it. And we cannot say, from any results that we have reached so far, that an examination of the facts of morality in human experience gives us any assurance that they are based on anything more than human nature. At most, the facts of morality might be one group of facts among many, all of which point to a particular conclusion about the nature of reality: as, for instance, it has been held that an examination of the nature of the judgment leads us to adopt a certain view about the nature of reality and, of course, moral judgments are one class of judgments, among others. But the facts of morality, if we have rightly understood them, cannot be assigned any special place as evidence, so that we could draw from them valid conclusions about the nature of reality, for which we found no evidence in anything else, still less conclusions which were opposed to those that would be drawn from the other evidence.

Our conclusion, then, is that our theory of the moral fact and the nature of morality does not depend upon any one particular theory about the nature of reality, nor can it be used as evidence which will establish any such theory. Such a theory would have to be proved on other, or at least very much wider grounds than could be found by an examination of the facts of morality. On the other hand, the view that we come to about the nature of reality may be of very great interest for our, or any other moral theory, as lending it additional confirmation and answering questions which the statement of our moral theory inevitably suggests. It would obviously be going very far outside the scope of this work to attempt even to summarize the general considerations which have been put forward in support of one view of the nature of reality or another. But we may state briefly some of the metaphysical theories which seem to work in well with our view of the nature of morality, in so far as they show how the moral processes which are an expression of the nature of humanity may at the same time be thought of as an expression of the nature of the whole of reality of which humanity is but a part. Our statements will necessarily be brief and inadequate, but they will serve to show how an ethical theory may be related to a wider metaphysical theory.

1. Take, first, the metaphysical theory which, in one form or another, is known as Absolutism. It is difficult to do justice even to the general features of this view in a few phrases. But, roughly, we may say that this view regards reality as a whole of connected and interdependent parts. The whole alone is completely real and the whole alone is completely intelligible. The parts of the whole, the different particular " things," have only a limited and fragmentary degree of reality, and judgments about them can only approximate more or less closely to the truth.

For such a view goodness in the moral sphere would be what truth is in the intellectual sphere (though, no doubt, such a distinction would only be admitted as valid relatively to our incomplete state of knowledge). That is to say, that goodness for the individual would lie in the extension of the individual self outside itself, in the increasing identification of the individual self with a wider whole, first and foremost, no doubt, a wider whole of other selves, and an increasing sense of unity with this. Evil would lie in exclusiveness, in cutting oneself off from other individuals and the rest of the wider whole.

Such a view would have no difficulty in accepting our account of the moral fact as relatively true at the level of knowledge at which we thought in terms of individual human beings. The ideal object of desire, as we have described it, would then be taken as an expression of the nature of truth and reality. The desire for the good would be a particular form of the striving towards reality, which would lead us to attempt to increase the closeness of our relations with other beings. And the chief forms in which this striving expressed itself might well be described, at our level of thought, by terms like love and knowledge. And the great evil would be, as our view has maintained, lack of love which led to selfishness and shutting out others from ourselves, which would be the negation of truth and reality, because it would be putting the part before the whole.

2. Another metaphysical doctrine, which, in some of its forms, is quite compatible with the last, and which has a similar bearing on our ethical theory, is the doctrine of Theism. Kant believed that the existence of the moral law in itself implied the existence of a supreme, perfectly good being. We could not accept his argument, as it stands : but it is clear that some form of theistic doctrine would form a very good metaphysical background to our ethical theory.

Our theory has explained morality by reference to conscious human beings. All forms of Theism maintain the existence of one supreme, eternal Being, endowed with consciousness, will, and the other general characteristics of conscious beings, as we know them, but with all these characteristics developed up to the highest pitch of their potentiality. Such a Supreme Being is thought of as having some kind of special relation to other conscious beings, so that in some way their wills are a partial expression of His will. The good, which is the object of their potential desire, as described, is the object of His active desire, and it is in virtue of their special relation to Him that they have this element in their nature. So, too, His nature is the standard of the good, and He is the actualization of what they would desire to become. It is also held, in most forms of theistic doctrine, that the Supreme Being not only has this relation to other conscious beings, but has also the same, or an analogous relation, to all the rest of reality, so that all the processes of physical nature in some way proceed from Him and are an expression of His will. Thus it is sometimes argued, in reinforcement of this view, that the will or purpose of some conscious being is the only really intelligible explanation of anything, the only completely satisfactory answer to the question, Why? If, therefore, a final explanation of the Universe is to be given at all, it can only be in terms of will or purpose.

It is, therefore, because it and we alike are in some way expressions of the Supreme Will of the Universe that we should desire the ideal if we understood what it was. It is thus a Law of Nature, in the highest and fullest sense, that such an ideal would be the supreme object of desire for any conscious being.

3. The doctrine of Theism thus secures what is sometimes supposed to be a necessity of any satisfactory moral theory, namely, a basis for the belief in the permanence of values. And another doctrine, which is supposed to secure the same results, is the doctrine of personal immortality. Thus, it is argued that moral values, like all values, depend upon a certain relation to a conscious mind or minds, so that without conscious minds there can be no values. And it is, therefore, held that, if moral values are to be permanent, the conscious minds which make them values must be permanent too.

If this is put forward, as it has been by some writers, as a necessary presupposition of morality, there certainly seems to be a logical hiatus in the argument. We have already suggested that the authority of moral values for us here and now does not depend, if our account of them is correct, on their being permanent. But, apart from this, there does not seem any necessity to postulate the continued existence of individual minds in order to secure the permanence of values. The demand for permanence is sufficiently met if we say not that individual human minds are permanent, but that Mind is permanent, in some form or other. We could say, for instance, that there will always be some conscious beings, or that there will always be one eternal supreme Mind. Either of these doctrines would be sufficient to secure the permanence of values, without it being necessary to suppose that each individual mind has a permanent existence.

It is difficult to see, on our view of morality, why it should be supposed to be dependent on a belief in personal immortality. Of course, on the view that the moral fact, the motive for doing what we thought to be right, consisted simply in the prospect of extrinsic rewards and punishments, it would, no doubt, be necessary to postulate a future life where these rewards and punishments would be distributed to us, because it is sufficiently obvious that they are not distributed according to merit in this life. Such a view, no doubt, would not be seriously put forward by anyone in this crude form at the present time. But, in a more refined form, a somewhat analogous view might be put forward consistently with our principles, if it were maintained that it was necessary to suppose a future life where the ideal situation, which was the supreme object of desire, would be realized and become actual. We cannot, however, consistently admit this necessity. It is clear that the mere fact of personal immortality would, by itself, give us no warrant for the belief that the ideal would be realized in the future life any more than in this life. It would be difficult or impossible to show that the realization of the ideal here was prevented simply and solely by the special conditions of this life, which we might expect to be altered in a life after physical death. And the question need not trouble us greatly, because it should be abundantly clear from what we have said of it that there is no necessity to maintain that the ideal will ever actually be realized in its completeness—for, of course, it is being continually realized in part—at any one point of time. Its validity as a regulative principle is not affected by this.

But all this is not to say that the question of personal immortality is entirely irrelevant from the moral point of view. The claim of the ideal upon us is the same whether we are immortal or not. And the general nature of the ideal is the same, too. But, as we know too well, in actual conduct it is not a question of realizing the ideal in its completeness, but of approaching as closely to it as we can. And the problem sometimes presents itself in practice in the form of a question about what we must sacrifice of the things which, in ideal circumstances, we should require. When it is a matter of practical policy of this kind, it is possible that our beliefs about personal immortality might affect our decision. For it seems at least probable that in certain circumstances our practical decisions might be different according as we believed that the ideal would have to be realized, so far as it ever could be realized, on this earth or not at all, or that the progress towards the ideal would be continued, in entirely different circumstances, in another life. We might find some sort of analogy to this difference in a question of educational policy. Many people would hold, for instance, that the best course of instruction at a school would be different for a pupil whose education was to end at the conclusion of his school days from what it would be for one who was going to continue it at a University. The analogy does not of course take us very far, but it serves to indicate the kind of difference that different opinions on the question of immortality might lead to in practice.

Very little serious attention has been given to this question. And, in the lack of previous discussion, it is difficult to do more than put forward a very tentative suggestion about the kind of situation in which our opinions about human immortality might affect our moral judgment. Imagine a man somewhat of the type of Arthur Hugh Clough, a man, that is to say, of great ability and great possibilities of influencing his fellow-beings for good, brought up in the orthodox faith of his time, who loses this faith in an age and a country in which a departure from orthodox opinions has the effect of putting a barrier between oneself and the vast majority of one's fellow-countrymen. Suppose that, like Clough, our imagined case is not of the robust stuff of which pioneers of new truth, who influence the thought of their generation, are made, so that the only effect of his loss of faith is to make him lose his bearings and to cut him off from the society in which he might have played a useful part. We may suppose that he has got nearer to the truth than he would have done had he remained in the faith of his fathers, but, for all that, looking at the whole effect on others besides himself, it is evident that the result of his loss of faith has been loss rather than gain. If, therefore, it was only a question of life on this earth, we should probably have to condemn such a life as wasted and ineffectual; and, if it was ever in our power to influence a man in such circumstances, we should probably feel it our duty to influence him against following the course which this man took.[1]

On the other hand, if we believed that there was a future life for him and others, we should recognize that what happened had at least secured that he started this future life nearer to the truth than he would otherwise have been. And we could at least have the hope that he might find himself in a situation where he could play a useful part in the social movement towards the ideal. In general, then, it seems possible that our solution of many problems in which it is a question of upsetting established beliefs, without the certainty of being able to provide an alternative, or of cutting oneself off in any way from the only society in which on this earth one could be a valuable influence, might be affected by our views on personal immortality, if we took them seriously. But any such conclusions can only, for the present, be taken as very tentative suggestions.

What, then, is our general conclusion on all these points? We have seen that our views on these different subjects may affect our views about moral questions in various ways. As in the last instance, they may affect our judgments and

[1] It is related of James Fitzjames Stephen that he stated that he should be sorry if any large portion of the human race held views like his own.

decisions on practical moral problems. They may strengthen and confirm our conclusions on moral questions, by showing how they fit in with our general metaphysical position. And all these subjects are such that reflection on moral problems cannot but suggest questions about them and stimulate us to carry our investigations in them further.

But this does not take us very far. The important question that we have to ask is, Are our general views on the problem of Ethics affected by our views on these questions, so that we have to make up our minds on these subjects before we can come to any conclusion on ethical matters? More particularly, is our belief in morality dependent on our holding any or all of these views? Is there no moral fact unless Absolutism or Theism or any of these doctrines is true? And, conversely, can the facts of morality be taken as a proof of or evidence for the truth of any of these views? If we adopt the account that we have given of the nature of the moral fact, we must answer in the negative to all these questions.

For consider. Our account of the moral fact is a deduction from the actual experience of human beings here on this earth, from their experience of morality, of moral judgments and moral actions. As an explanation of these facts, we have inferred certain facts about our human nature, namely, that it is such that we should desire the ideal before all else if we only grasped what it really was. As we have already pointed out, our ground for confidence in the validity of our inferences was that they were inferences about our own nature, and could therefore reasonably be inferred from our own experience. But all these metaphysical theories go beyond these facts and beyond judgments about our own nature here and now. And if our conclusions go beyond this, the ground for confidence in the validity of our inferences from these facts disappears.

Or, to look at it from the other end, our account of the moral fact is put forward as a hypothesis which explains certain obvious facts of experience which cannot be denied. Of course, any metaphysical theory which involved a denial of these facts would stand condemned. Such a theory is perhaps possible, but there is no question of it in any of the doctrines that we have been considering. The question that must be raised is whether, supposing that we denied any of these theories, that would involve either denying these facts or invalidating the inferences that we have drawn from them. And it is impossible to see any reason why it should. Therefore, it is clear that we must look to other considerations to enable us to decide whether these metaphysical doctrines are true or false. And when, on these other grounds, we have arrived at a positive metaphysical doctrine about the nature of Reality, we can proceed to ask how our particular ethical theory fits into it, and what relation it bears to the rest of the doctrine. Such an investigation would be of the highest interest and importance. But it comes after we have arrived at a conclusion on ethical questions, and our ethical theory does not depend for its validity on any one of these metaphysical doctrines.

These same considerations apply to another question, which is essentially metaphysical, but which has often been thought to have a special bearing on ethical problems; and that is the question of the freedom of the will. This question is essentially metaphysical, because it involves an examination of one of the most general categories, namely, the category of causation, and an answer to the question whether, or in what sense, this relation runs through the whole of reality. More particularly, it involves an answer to the question whether the category of causation as used in the physical sciences does or does not apply to human action. If it does not, this would seem to necessitate the recognition of a fundamental distinction between these two orders of being: and questions like this about the different modes of being are the subject-matter of Metaphysics.

But it has been held that a decision on this metaphysical

question was an essential preliminary to a decision on the main problem of Ethics. For without freedom, it was held, there could be no such thing as morality. Kant, in the famous phrase, "I ought, therefore I can," expresses his belief in the fundamental connexion between freedom and morality. And he held, not only that morality implied freedom, but further that this established freedom as a fact. For he regarded moral judgments as of such certainty and authority that their testimony outweighed any logical or speculative difficulties that there might be in the idea of freedom, and impelled us to believe in it and justified this belief.

Our view, however, does not warrant any such conclusion, nor, indeed, does it necessitate a decision one way or the other on the question of human freedom. On our view, if we say that an action is right or good, we mean either that it will have certain results, or, more properly, that it proceeds from a certain state of mind or a certain character. The question of freedom in the end comes down to a discussion about the nature of the relation between the state of mind or the character and the action. No one denies that there is a relation and indeed a very close connexion. An absolutely isolated action, out of all relation to the character or the personality of the agent is really unthinkable, and certainly could not possibly be the subject of a moral judgment. But what the full nature of this relation is, whether, for instance, it is exactly the same as the relation which we call causal between two events in the physical series, can only be a matter for metaphysical speculation. Our theory of the moral fact does not enable us to pronounce one way or the other on this question, nor does it necessitate any attempt to do so. It is sufficient for us that there is such a connexion.

CHAPTER XVI

MORAL THEORY AND MORAL PRACTICE (I)

WE may conclude our investigations by some attempt to answer the question, which is sure to be asked, What is the use of Moral Philosophy? Or, to put it more explicitly, What influence will whatever moral theory we arrive at have on our actual conduct? In particular, we must ask what difference the moral theory, which we have outlined above, will make to us in practice.

In this connexion, we must be careful to avoid the danger to which moral philosophers are particularly exposed, of making extravagant claims for the practical value of our particular theory. It would be foolish to claim for it, for instance, that it can, to put it bluntly, make a bad man good. That is to say, if there was a man who had no notion of an ideal and felt no conscious desire towards it, who was never moved by anything that we could call a moral impulse, and who never experienced any emotion of approval or disapproval, no theory of Moral Philosophy would give him these feelings that he lacked. We could tell such a man, if we liked, that he would desire the ideal, if he only had complete knowledge of it. But that will not make him desire it here and now, that will not make his potential desire actual, which is the great practical problem of morals. Nor, indeed, should we be able to make him accept even the theory. For an explanation of the facts of morality will not mean anything to him, unless he has some knowledge in his own experience of the facts to be explained. If he has no experience of these facts, if he resolutely denies their existence, then it is not possible to make him accept any particular explanation of them. Aristotle puts this point quite clearly, when he insists that some degree of formed moral disposition is necessary before we can begin a theoretical investigation into the nature of the moral fact.

In an extreme case like this, a moral theory can be of no help at all. But the problem presented by such a case is really altogether outside the special problem which is the subject of this chapter. Our special problem is to discover what effect our theory will have on practice, if it is accepted, and in the case imagined we have not even got to the point where the theory is accepted. But there is another case where, even if the theory is accepted, we cannot claim a direct practical effect for it. That is the case, which interested Aristotle, of the weak-willed man, the man who knows what is right and, in some sense, wants to do it, but never has the strength of will to resist temptation, when it comes his way. Such a case presents a very difficult problem, both practical and theoretical. No theoretical explanation of the moral fact will help a man like this, because he already knows, or may know, perfectly well both what is good and what good is. He may be as convinced as we are of the accuracy of our account of the general nature and content of the ideal situation: but that will not help him when temptation comes.

It has sometimes been supposed that the particular difficulty in a case like this lies in the lack of imagination, an incapacity to picture to oneself the real nature of the good and the evil alternatives, so that the good does not exercise the attractive force that it would if its nature were fully realized. But, though such cases are undoubtedly frequent, this hardly seems a satisfactory explanation of the special case that we are considering. For the typical weak-willed person has very often an extremely vivid imagination, so that he is quite capable of picturing to himself the ideal situation, desires it passionately, and feels proportionate depths of remorse when, by some act of his own, he hinders its attainment. It would appear, rather, that his particular weakness consists in a defect of attention. He imagines vividly the ideal situation and sees clearly what he has lost by his own action, when he thinks of it, but at the moment of action he does not or cannot keep his mind fixed on the thought of the ideal, so that it fails to arouse an active desire for it in him at that moment. His attention is fixed rather on the pleasurable elements in the temptation to which he yields. No particular theory can help him here or affect this weakness of his. It is possible that such a theory, if true, may help him indirectly, in so far as it describes the conditions of his special problem correctly, and by doing that takes the first step to finding a solution for it, if a solution can ever be found. But beyond this it certainly cannot go.

There is, perhaps, one possible case where a moral theory might have a direct practical effect of this kind, if it were accepted. We might suppose the case of a man who began with real moral impulses and a real desire for the good, but later was influenced by various theories and arguments which seemed to show that there was no moral fact and which attempted to explain away the glimpses that he thought he had had of it. If he became convinced of this, he would see that there was no possible reason for action, except the desires which he actually felt, and that there was no way of discovering what would really satisfy him except through an examination of these desires. And he might well come to the conclusion that these moral impulses, if they ever came into conflict with his selfish desires, had no claim to superiority over them, and should, for his own comfort, be suppressed. If such a man, while he was in process of falling under the influence of these anti-moral theories, was presented with a theory which seemed to offer a reasonable explanation of the moral fact, so that he could rationally continue to believe in it, it might save him from proceeding further with these theories, and so affect his action.

It is, however, doubtful whether, in this extreme form, such a case could ever actually occur. If a man really started with first-hand moral experience, it is not very easy to believe that he could ever be so carried away by arguments of this kind that he would thus turn his back on his own experience. It is much more probable that he would simply say that these theories did not explain the facts, and refuse to accept them, even if he was not capable himself of working out a satisfactory alternative theory. But, in a minor degree, it does seem possible that arguments and theories on moral questions might exercise some influence of this kind in one direction or another. And, in so far as they could, the exposition of a satisfactory moral theory might be of some help in removing obstacles to a man's belief in what his moral experience would make him wish to believe. But the extent of this influence would be very intangible and difficult to estimate correctly.

With this possible but in any case insignificant exception, it would seem that we cannot expect a moral theory to have any direct effect in the way of providing people with a motive to right action, if they have not such a motive already. But that is not the service which it is most commonly supposed that a moral theory ought to perform, if it is to be considered of any value for actual conduct. It would not often be put forward as a reproach against any theory that it did not by itself provide a motive for action. But there is a further possibility. If we suppose a person who wants to do right, but often finds it difficult to decide in particular cases what is the right thing to do, we may well ask whether our moral theory would help him. Would it tell him what particular action or kind of action was right, if he were in any doubt? That was the claim made by Kant for his system of Moral Philosophy. He believed that his account of the nature of the moral fact would provide an infallible criterion in practice, by which we could say with certainty in any particular case whether an action was right or wrong. But it would probably be universally recognized now that this claim of his was not justified, and that, even if we accepted the main features of his theoretical account, the supposed practical criterion that it gave was entirely illusory.

On Aristotle's view of Moral Philosophy, which in this respect is ours, we could not even make this claim. For his view involves the denial of the idea that it is in any way possible to get absolute general rules by the use of which we can tell beforehand whether any particular sort of action will be right or wrong. To get general rules at all it is, of course, necessary to distinguish the common features of a number of different actions from their special individual features, to consider the former by themselves, and to ignore the latter. We must be able to say beforehand that any other elements that we may find in any particular action, over and above those general features which we have already distinguished and classified, are morally irrelevant, so that we can know without further knowledge of the particular action that we are justified in ignoring them. But this, on our theory, is just what we cannot do in moral, or indeed in any practical questions. We can never say for certain beforehand that any one of the special circumstances of an action is irrelevant to the question of its rightness or wrongness. And therefore we can never lay down beforehand, without considering the circumstances of each case, absolute general rules about what actions should or should not be done.

To avoid the possibility of confusion, it would be as well to point out that this only applies when we are considering actions from the point of view of the practical question of what we are to do. When we are judging an action already done, it is true to say, as we have seen, that its goodness depends entirely upon the fact that it proceeds from a certain state of mind, which we can describe in general terms, and that, therefore, the other circumstances about the action are, in a sense, morally irrelevant. But, even when judging of actions already done, this does not give us an infallible criterion which we can apply to any particular action that we may want to judge, so that we can say at once without possibility of error that it is good or bad. For, at any rate, in judging of the actions of other people, we have to infer the state of mind of the agent from the external features of the action. And we cannot say in general terms, without examining the circumstances of each particular case, what external features afford the most convincing evidence of a certain state of mind. And still less, when it is a question of deciding for ourselves what we ought to do, will a knowledge of the state of mind which makes an action good tell us, by itself, the particular kind of action in which the state of mind will express itself in all circumstances. Once more, we have to take all the circumstances of each case into account, and as no two cases are precisely the same in all circumstances, we cannot have any absolute universal rules of conduct.

We must, then, finally abandon all ideas of finding an infallible practical criterion in our ethical theory. Are we, then, to say that our ethical theory has no practical bearing at all? Far from it. It is a very common fallacy in this connexion to think that we are limited to two possible alternatives—on the one hand, the alternative of claiming that our ethical theory will provide us with an absolute and infallible code of rules for practical guidance, and on the other, that of admitting that it is of no practical value or importance whatever. This is a fallacy, because these two alternatives do not by any means exhaust the possibilities. An ethical theory, even if it does not give us a practical criterion of this kind, may be of enormous practical importance as giving us a general point of view from which to approach particular moral problems. For any particular case, the answer to the question, Is this action right or wrong? depends on an examination in detail of all the circumstances of that case. And nothing can dispense us from the necessity of this examination. But an ethical theory will tell us what we mean by the question, so that we can know what we must look for and how we are to proceed in our examination of this material : and that is an essential preliminary to getting a right answer to the question. We cannot hope to find a right answer to the question, except

MORAL THEORY AND MORAL PRACTICE (I) 199

by a happy accident, until we know exactly what the question means, what the methods are by which we can hope to answer it, how we can test the worth of our answers, what amount of certainty we have a right to expect, and many other points, the solutions of which in themselves constitute an ethical theory.

Thus, for instance, the very fact which our theory establishes that it is impossible to get absolute general rule of conduct gives us negative information of first-rate practical importance. It tells us that we cannot simply approve or condemn an action, as we are so often inclined to do, by merely referring it to some general rule. In the famous case, discussed by Kant, of the man pursued by murderers, whose life we could save by a timely lie, we cannot simply condemn the action by saying that it is wrong because it would be to tell a lie, and it is wrong to tell lies. On our view, we cannot thus save ourselves trouble by this simple method, and shirk the task of examining carefully all the details of the particular case.

On the other hand, we must beware of falling into the opposite error and talking as if it were impossible to make any general statements about conduct at all. We do perfectly legitimately lay down certain general rules of conduct: but we must always bear in mind that such rules can only be laid down with the reservation that they only hold, to use Aristotle's phrase, " for the most part." We mean, that is to say, that in the vast majority of cases conduct of one particular kind is right or wrong: it is, for instance, in all but very exceptional circumstances, wrong to tell a lie. And we can say more than that, in some cases. We can say, for instance in this particular case, that conduct of that kind is in itself wrong, because it could find no place and would be impossible in an ideal situation. Lying is incompatible with the realization of the ideal, because it is depriving another person of the knowledge which he would have in ideal circumstances and because it is putting a barrier of lack of trust and confidence between two or more people, which we could not believe would be there in the ideal situation. But, for all that, circumstances may arise in which the situation would be worse if we did not tell the lie than if we did. There are other cases in which the connexion between the action and the ideal is less immediate, where we think of the action as more nearly indifferent in itself and of importance simply as a means to bringing about an ideal state of things. But here, too, we may say that in all but very exceptional circumstances a certain kind of action will help to produce the state of things which we should desire. Many so-called political principles are of this kind. The principle, however, is the same in both cases. The accumulated moral experience of mankind has expressed itself in a more or less general code of moral rules and practical maxims, which express what has been found as a general rule most conducive to a good result. We must always be very careful how we break these rules, and anyone who does so incurs a heavy responsibility. But there may always be rare and exceptional circumstances in which it is right to break them. And we cannot evade the responsibility of examining carefully all the circumstances of each case by a mere appeal to the general rule.

To a certain extent the same principles apply when we are making decisions about and passing judgments on human character. This also may be a practical question. In the work of education, for instance, we are always likely to be faced with questions about what sort of character we want to develop. And, indeed, whenever it is a question of an action which may influence the development of a character, our own or another's, we must eventually come face to face with this problem. We have to consider what effect of this kind the action is likely to have. But more fundamental than that is the question whether we approve of this effect or not. Here, of course, we can say quite definitely that certain developments of character are always and necessarily bad, because they conflict directly with some element in the ideal. Under no conceivable circumstances, for instance, could one approve of the development of a strain of cruelty in a character. We have also a general idea of the ideal character, so that we can say that any feature in that character is good as far as it goes. But in practice we have to be careful in the application of this. The ideal character includes different elements. And, though in its complete development the different elements may involve each other, at the limited stage of development, which is all that the ordinary human being can hope to attain, this is not necessarily so. Perfect love and perfect knowledge, perhaps, can only exist together. But we know that in imperfect human beings there can be a considerable development of one of these elements without a corresponding development of the other.

The practical danger here is that we may concentrate too exclusively on one element in the ideal character and neglect the rest. And the value of Aristotle's doctrine of the Mean is that it puts us on our guard against this danger. In the light of these considerations we must conclude that, though we may say that a particular characteristic is good, because it would appear in the ideal character, we cannot say with absolute certainty that any action which tends to develop this characteristic is always and necessarily good. For there may be circumstances in which the action or course of action which would best develop this characteristic could only do so at the expense of some other element equally necessary to the perfect character. If we think only of the development of love and forget the necessity for knowledge, we may find that we have only succeeded in producing ": sloppy " sentimentality or blind, uncritical enthusiasms. And the development of knowledge without love would even more obviously fall short of our ideal. Any system of education which fell into either of these extremes would have to be condemned. In practice, we must balance the claims of these two constituent elements in the ideal character and avoid paying a too exclusive attention to either.

This is an illustration by means of a special case of what is the great practical moral problem, namely, the application of the ideal to practice. As we have seen, whatever may be the ultimate possibilities, we cannot think of the ideal as a situation which we can actually hope to realize here and now. It is rather an element in our actual lives of which we must try to attain as much as possible. And, in practice, we may often find ourselves obliged to sacrifice some part of the ideal, something which in ideal circumstances would be attained. It is constantly a matter of a choice of evils.

As a practical guide in these matters, we really need to formulate two ideals for ourselves. There is the final ideal, by reference to which everything else is to be judged, and there is the practical ideal, the best possible that we can hope to attain in the circumstances. The latter, of course, is derived from the former and owes any validity it has to it. We have to arrive at it, to a certain extent, by elimination, by deciding what we must forgo. But our notion of it will also have to contain much more detail than our notion of the final ideal. For, as we have seen, in this latter we cannot include any special external circumstances. In a very general way, we can exclude certain possible conditions as being incompatible with the ideal. But we cannot say that any particular circumstances are necessarily contained in the ideal situation. On the other hand, when we try to formulate a practical ideal, we must be clear about the external conditions which we are aiming at. We must decide what are the alterations in the actual circumstances which we may hope to bring about and which will best conduce to the realization of as much as possible of the final ideal. All this is work which each man must do for himself. No ethical theory can give infallible practical guidance here. But it can show us what the real problem is: and this is an essential precondition of its solution.

Besides this, there is another way in which our ethical

theories may affect our practical conduct, by giving us a general point of view from which to look at the practical problems that present themselves. We have already seen how in our ordinary moral thinking we often contradict ourselves, so that in practice we may decide similar problems sometimes one way and sometimes another. This condition of confusion is obviously bad, whatever theory we may ultimately adopt. And in searching for a theory and considering all the evidence which may help us to find one, we cannot help noticing these contradictions, and, to a great extent at any rate, getting rid of them. To construct a theory at all, we must at least make an effort to be consistent, and in the process of constructing a theory, whatever theory it may be, we shall at least have to face the problems raised by contradictions in our ordinary thought, and by doing this go some way towards solving them. Even if our solution is wrong, we have at least clarified our thinking, and that is an essential step in the direction of finding the right solution.

CHAPTER XVII

MORAL THEORY AND MORAL PRACTICE (II)

THERE remains still one further way in which philosophical speculation on moral problems may affect our conduct. And a brief consideration of this will conclude our investigations.

We have dealt hitherto almost exclusively with the philosophical criticism of the most general and fundamental moral categories, such as " good " and " right." But these are not the only moral categories, and the philosophical attitude of mind is not restricted to an examination of these. It will also pay attention to what we may call the subordinate moral categories, which equally demand criticism : and we are now in a position to apply such criticism in the light of the results we have already reached. To say a thing is good or right is not the only form of moral judgment. We also judge of actions or individual characters as fair or just or courageous or generous, implying by the use of these terms that such an action or such a character is right or good because it possesses one or other of these qualities. But our ordinary notions of the true meaning of these terms are no more free from confusion and obscurity than our notion of the meaning of the more general moral categories. A critical examination of them would be a necessary part of a complete system of Ethics. Such an examination is essayed by Aristotle, not perhaps with conspicuous success, in his account of the particular virtues. As we are not attempting to construct a complete ethical system, we need not attempt a complete examination of all these subordinate moral categories. We may be content with some brief illustrations of the way in which the application of philosophical criticism to these particular virtues might have some effect on our moral practice.

We often say, for instance, that we ought not to act in such-and-such a way because it would not be fair or not be just. And this often presents no difficulty. But there are occasions on which our ordinary ways of thinking seem to set up justice as a principle of morality that can override everything else. As the proverb, *Fiat justitia, ruat coelum*, seems to imply, we think that an act can be judged as just or unjust, and therefore right or wrong, quite apart from its consequences or its relation to anything else. Particularly in public affairs do we seem to come across cases of apparent conflict between the principle of justice and the good of the community. Consider, for instance, an institution like that of Ostracism in ancient Athens. There it was possible from time to time to take a vote of the whole people on the question whether it was in the interests of the community that any particular citizen should be expelled from the city for a term of years: and if sufficient votes were cast against any one man, he was banished. No crime was alleged against him, and indeed it was not considered a punishment. It was a step taken in the public interest, which was superior to the claims of any one citizen.

Now, most of us could probably think of one or more prominent public men of the present time whose banishment for a term of years would probably be in the best interests of the community. Yet no one at the present time would seriously propose the establishment of an institution like that of Ostracism in any form. Of course, simply from the point of view of the national interest, it would be possible to find decisive arguments against it. It might be argued, for instance, that it would be impossible to find anybody whose judgment was so infallible that they could safely be entrusted with the decision in a matter like this. They would be just as likely, or even more likely, to banish a man whose presence really was of value to the nation, because of some prejudice they had against him. But it is probable that that is not the first objection which would occur to the majority of people. Their first impulse would be to say that, even if the sentence of banishment were really in the highest interests of the community, it would not be fair to the individual man to inflict this penalty on him, except as a recognized legal punishment for a definite crime.

Another instance of a somewhat different kind might be suggested. During the late war it was often necessary to find men to fill certain posts of a more or less technical nature, in which special knowledge and special qualifications were necessary, or at least highly desirable. Such posts were often well paid and comparatively safe and comfortable. From the point of view of winning the war, and, assuming that it was in the general interest that we should win the war, from the point of view of the general interest, the obvious thing to do was to fill these posts with the men best qualified to hold them. But to many people, particularly to those who did not possess any of those special qualifications, it seemed very unfair that those who did possess them should escape the dangers and discomforts which other people had to go through. And it was often urged, sometimes with success, that these particular posts should be given as a reward for long and meritorious service, or at least that the men with the special qualifications should only receive them after they had " done their turn in the trenches."

Now, it is clear that on our principles this point of view is absolutely unjustifiable. We have the single standard of the ideal by which everything is to be judged. And, whatever justice may be, it derives any validity it has as a moral principle of action from its relation to this ideal, and it cannot be set up as a rival with equal claims of its own. If we think, taking everything into account, that an action will really help towards the attainment of the ideal, then that action must be done, whatever people may think about its justice. If an unjust action is always and necessarily wrong, then we must say that no action which tends towards the realization of the ideal can be unjust. If we ever say that it is, then we must mean that justice is another principle of action which may sometimes conflict with the supreme moral principle, and then we should have to say that, in certain circumstances, an unjust action might be good, and a just action bad.

To give a complete account of all that justice ever means in popular usage and all that it might mean within the limits of our theory would be a task beyond our present scope. But some brief suggestions may be made as to the truth which underlies our ordinary ideas of it, and which is at the back even of the erroneous views that we have just considered.

Considered in the light of the ideal, the true principle of justice is an expression of the fact that each human being is, and should be treated as, an end in himself, and never as a mere means. This is, of course, Kant's second maxim, and is here expressed in Kantian language to show how it is possible for two lines of thought, starting from very different principles, to arrive at the same result in their application. For this maxim follows just as certainly from our principles as from Kant's. The ideal situation, of course, to be complete must include everyone, and we cannot arbitrarily select any individual to be left out of it. But further than that it is clear that perfect love for a person involves treating that person as an end, and never as a means. We could not say that we truly loved anybody if we regarded them simply as a means to the gratification of the wishes of ourselves or of any other individual. No doubt, we could say in a sense—though it would be rather misleading—that each individual was really a means to the realization of the ideal for the totality of individuals. But, of course, each individual is included in this totality, and therefore is never merely a means. And this principle, so far as it is true, applies equally to all individuals. There is no question of preferring the interests of one individual, simply as an individual, to those of another. In the ideal situation everyone is on an equality.

This does not mean that everyone here and now must be

treated exactly the same. And as the ideal is never attainable in its completeness at any time, there may arise the question of sacrificing even the real good of one individual to secure the greater good of others. But it does mean that, as everyone is equally an end, we must apply whatever principles of action we adopt impartially as between man and man. If in practice we make a difference in our treatment of different people, we must be guided solely by reference to the ideal and not by any other motive. Thus, for instance, if facilities for education and the acquisition of knowledge are limited by circumstances which we cannot alter, it is clear that some people will have to do without the best education possible, and so far their highest interests must be sacrificed. But if we have to take part in deciding who is to be sacrificed, we must be guided solely by the consideration, Whose education will best conduce to the greatest possible realization of the ideal in the actual circumstances? We must never, for instance, allow ourselves to be influenced by our personal predilection for one individual as against another.

This points to a certain possibility of danger in the practical application of our doctrine, against which the insistence on the importance of the principle of justice may act as a warning. The danger is that, if we think too much of love as the supreme good and forget the limitations of our imperfect love, we may come to treat the actual love which we feel as our sole guide in action, so that we treat those whom we know and love on quite a different footing to those whom we do not know or love less, even to the extent of regarding the latter simply as a means to the satisfaction of the desires of the former. Action which involves that is bad, although in a sense it proceeds from a sentiment of love, because it is really the result not merely of love for one person or a limited number of people but also of a deficiency of love for others, and a lack of imaginative sympathy with those outside our immediate acquaintance.

We must remember that the love which in the full sense

we can only feel for a limited number of people is not the only moral motive, and is not by itself a sufficient guide in practice. There is also the desire to realize the ideal as fully as possible, to spread love and knowledge throughout the world among those whom we can never know and therefore never love in the full sense. This desire itself is an expression of love in the more restricted sense which we have already mentioned. Or we might say that it is an expression of the potential love that we should feel in ideal circumstances, without which we could not be completely satisfied if we really understood what we were missing. And the recognition that this has a superior claim even to the love that we actually feel for individual people expresses itself in the form of a recognition of the importance of the principle of justice.

The principle of justice, then, appears in its proper place as an expression of the desire for the ideal. But we also attach importance to it as a practical principle of action, which lays down the kind of action which is the best means to the attainment of the ideal. Thus we saw how special circumstances may make it right to treat one person on a different footing from another. But, in many cases, even when we admit the necessity of doing this, we still feel uneasy about it. And it is easy to explain why we feel thus, and why it is really desirable that we should feel thus.

This is really a special case of what we have already noted in discussing the possibility and value of general rules of conduct. We feel that justice, as meaning equality of treatment, expresses the spirit of the ideal. That is the result of the moral experience of generations. And, even if we admit that there may be cases in which we should depart from this principle, we still very often feel a doubt whether any one of us, with our limited knowledge, is really competent to decide whether such a case is actually before us. We may admit all that has been said to the effect that absolute equality of treatment is impossible, because no two cases are ever actually alike. But for all that we feel that, if the obvious features of two cases are alike, it is safer in practice to treat them as the same, because our knowledge of the other features is so very scanty and our opinion about them so uncertain. So that we feel that it is safer to stick to a fixed principle of action, even if that involves acting wrongly in a few cases, because we should probably make many more mistakes if we tried to act on our own discretion in each case.

It is impossible not to feel the force of these considerations, even if opinions might differ as to the exact extent of the limitations of human reason which they imply. But, on the other hand, there is also a danger in the other direction. For these considerations may be taken simply as an excuse for intellectual laziness, and as a reason for shirking the task of thinking out and examining the conditions and circumstances of each case, thus leading to an unintelligent and unprogressive formalism and insistence on the letter of the law. Each of us has to decide for himself which of these opposing dangers he considers the more serious. But our theoretical consideration has advanced so far that it has given us a statement of the problem which we have to solve for ourselves.

There are many other ways in which a criticism of these subordinate moral categories may affect our moral practice. There may be times or circumstances in which one particular virtue has an exaggerated importance attached to it, so that people may come to think that the presence of that virtue is sufficient justification of any action or of anyone's character, and forget to inquire what the proper place of that virtue is in the ideal situation. Thus in time of war we are very likely to attach an excessive value to the virtue of courage, and to think that any other quality is of small account beside it. Courage, if we mean by it a power of resistance to the impulses of the emotion of fear, is no doubt an essential condition of the ideal state of mind. We cannot work for the attainment of the ideal nor can we act as the ideal state of mind would lead us to act if we are always liable to be overcome by the emotion of fear so that we forget our own object and only act as the emotion drives us to act. But, on the other hand, considered in the light of our principles courage appears as only one among many elements in the ideal state of mind, and it is difficult to see how it can be considered of any moral value by itself, if it is used in the pursuit of other, perhaps unworthy ends. Or again, in similar circumstances, patriotism may be exalted to the position of the supreme virtue, to which all others are subordinate. And certainly in so far as it means that the individual must sacrifice his own comfort and pleasures and safety, if necessary, for the welfare of the whole nation, patriotism is an expression of the ideal point of view. But if it is extended to mean that the rights and interests of anyone outside our own nation have no sort of claim on us and may be rightly neglected, it is difficult to see how, on our principles, it can be defended.

Perhaps the most striking instances of the way in which philosophical criticism might affect our opinions and through them our actions are to be found in the domain of political thought, and it is there that there seems most need for an application of this criticism. We are all familiar with the way in which political arguments are based on the use of certain categories, generally very imperfectly criticized. Thus we constantly hear the statement that such-and-such a policy or measure is right or wrong because it is democratic or undemocratic or because it increases or diminishes liberty. And we find conceptions like democracy and liberty appealed to by people of the most different shades of opinion, and sometimes by the opposite sides in a particular controversy. It is clear that the full meaning of these categories has not in such cases been realized, and systematic criticism of them could not but affect the opinions, and through them the actions, which were based on their application. It is because there has been so little philosophical criticism in this field that most people are so helpless in the presence of general political ideas, and so easily aroused to unthinking enthusiasm or equally unthinking panic by the mere use of a phrase. And, after all, all this is merely a particular case of the general truth, that our actions are affected, at any rate, to some extent, by our opinions, and our opinions are affected by the degree of clearness with which we understand the full meaning of the categories that we employ in arriving at them. And that is how Philosophy can and must influence our actual conduct.

These few suggestions bring us to the end of our investigations. But, in Philosophy, the end of one task can only be thought of as the beginning of the next. We have stated the problem of Moral Philosophy. We have examined briefly some attempts to solve it. And, on the basis of this examination, we have arrived at some positive ideas of our own. But such results as we have attained at every turn suggest fresh problems to us. We want to know, for instance, much more about the different metaphysical views about the nature of reality, on which our particular ethical views could hope to find a firm foundation. We want a much fuller psychological account of what goes on in the mind of actual men and women when they judge on moral grounds or act from moral motives. And we want to see our principles applied in much greater detail, so that we can see how they explain all the particular moral judgments that we make and all the principles of moral conduct on which we base our actions. These are only some of the demands that occur to us: and if we satisfied them that would only raise further questions to be solved. For there is no end and no limit to philosophical speculation. And the aim of a single work cannot be to provide an answer to all the questions that can be asked. It has fulfilled its purpose and justified itself if it serves to stimulate those who read it to further investigation in the great problems with which it deals.

BIBLIOGRAPHY OF SOME RECENT BOOKS ON ETHICS

Bibliography of Some Recent Books on Ethics

Baier, K., *The Moral Point of View* (Ithaca, N.Y., 1958)
Brandt, R. B., *Ethical Theory* (Englewood Cliffs, N.J., 1959)
Ewing, A. C., *Ethics* (London, 1953)
Frankena, W. K., *Ethics* (Englewood Cliffs, N.J., 1963)
Garnett, A. C., *The Moral Nature of Man* (New York, 1952)
Hare, R. M., *The Language of Morals* (Oxford, 1952)
    Freedom and Reason (Oxford, 1963)
Nowell-Smith, P. H., *Ethics* (London, 1954)
Singer, M., *Generalization in Ethics* (New York, 1961)
Stevenson, C. L., *Ethics and Language* (New Haven, 1944)
von Wright, G. H., *Norm and Action* (London, 1963)
Melden, A. I. (ed.), *Ethical Theories: a Book of Readings* (Englewood Cliffs, N.J., 1955)

INDEX

Abbott, Dr. T. K., 45
Absolutism, 184 f.
Action, 19
Action, Aristotle on, 89 f.
—— and knowledge, 47 f., 91 f.
—— and motive, 169
——, neutral, 173
—— and production, 98 f.
——, voluntary, 89
Activity, Aristotle on, 94 f., 143, 149
"Agathos," 7 f., 68
"Aidos," 138
Aristotle, 47 f., 65 f., 194, 197
—— and Kant, 82, 86
—— on action, 89 f.
——   activity, 94 f., 143, 149
——   contemplation, 102 f.
——, *Ethics*, 70
—— on evil, 101
——   excellence, 79 f.
——   function, 74 f.
——   God, 104
——   good, 111 f.
——   goodness, 80 f.
——   happiness, 72 f., 98 f.
——   incontinence, 91
——   the mean, 81 f., 201
——, *Metaphysics*, 104
—— on moral categories, 204
——   pleasure, 73, 77, 94 f., 149
——   reason and feeling, 86
——   reason and intellect, 79
——   universality, 82
Autonomy, 33

Beauty, 102, 154
Bosanquet, Dr. B., 97
Butler, Bishop, 63, 163
—— on conscience, 63

Categorical imperative, 29
Categories, moral, 1, 204, 210
Character, development of, 200 f.
Choice, 89
Clough, A. H., 188
Conscience, 4, 138, 175 f.
——, Butler on, 63
——, Mill on, 59
Contemplation, 108, 144, 148
——, Aristotle on, 102 f.
Courage, 210
Criterion, practical, 198
Criticism, philosophical, 1
Custom and morality, 166

Desire, 117 f.
—— for good, 129 f.
——, ideal object of, 141 f.

Desire in experience, 137
——, Kant on, 50
——, potential, 133
Duty, Kant on, 29 f.

End, 48 f., 71 f., 98 f., 207
—— and means, 177
Ends, Kingdom of, 32 f.
Environment, 5, 171
Eudemus, 104
Evil, 100 f., 184
Excellence, Aristotle on, 79
Experience, æsthetic, 154
——, desire in, 137
—— in psychology, 131, 161

Fact, moral, 12, 132 f., 136, 158 f.
Fallacy of Kant, 46 f., 51 f., 106
——, psychological, 131, 139
Feeling and reason, 86, 155 f.
——, moral, 163 f.
Freedom, 33
——, Kant on, 192
—— of the will, 191 f.
Function, Aristotle on, 74 f.

God, Aristotle on, 104
Good, 3, 8, 9, 51, 106 f., 111 f., 136, 179
—— and desire, 129 f.
—— as universal, 25
——, Greek use of term, 68
——, Kant on, 19
Goodness, Aristotle on, 80 f.
——, Moore, Mr. G. E., on, 52
——, Sidgwick, H., on, 60 f.
—— and rightness, 180
Gorgias, 68
Greek politics, 72
—— State, 69, 72
—— use of "Good," 68

Happiness, 90, 108 f.
——, Aristotle on, 72 f., 98 f.
Hedonism, 64, 94 f., 149
Heteronomy, 33
Honour, 73
Hypothetical imperative, 29

Ideal, knowledge and the, 148
——, moral, 164, 181, 202
—— object of desire, 141 f.
—— of character, 201
——, practical, 202
——, social, 143
Immortality, 186
Imperative, categorical **and** hypothetical, 29

Imperatives, Kant on, 28 f.
Intuition, 83

JUDGMENT, 161
Judgments, moral, 10, 158 f., 169
Justice, 205 f.

KANT, 15 f.
—— and Aristotle, 82, 86
——, assumptions of, 17 f.
——, *Metaphysic of Morals*, 15 f.
——, method of, 16
—— on desire, 50
——   duty, 29 f.
——   freedom, 192
——   good, 19
——   imperative, 28 f.
——   knowledge, 26
——   Law, 20 f., 27 f.
——   moral law, 27 f., 32 f.
——   practice, 196
——   pure self, 34 f.
——   reason, 27
——   respect, 21
——   Theism, 185
——   Will, 19 f., 28, 32
Kingdom of Ends, 32 f.
Knowledge and action, 47 f., 91 f.
—— and the ideal, 148
——, Kant on, 26

LAW, Kant on, 20 f., 27 f.
——, —— on the moral, 27 f., 32 f.
Love, 144 f., 151 f., 169, 174, 208

MACDOUGALL, Dr. W., 155
Maxims of Kant, 23, 28, 31 f., 42 f., 207
Mean, 113, 201
——, Aristotle on the, 81 f., 201
Means and Ends, 177
Metaphysic of Morals, 15 f.
Metaphysics, 181 f.
Metaphysics, Aristotle, 104
Mill, J. S., 58 f., 90, 138, 168
——, —— on conscience, 59
Moore, Mr. G. E., 52 f.
Moral categories, 1, 204, 210
—— fact, 12, 132 f., 136, 158 f.
—— feelings, 163 f.
—— ideal, 164, 181, 202
—— judgments, 10, 158 f., 169
—— law, Kant on the, 27 f., 32 f.
—— philosophy, 1, 6 f., 193 f.
—— practice, 5, 193 f.
—— value, 179
—— worth, 4, 20
Morality and custom, 166
Motives, 19, 137, 168
Murray, Prof. G., 138

NECESSITY, 33, 41

OBLIGATION, 28, 67 f.
Ostracism, 205
"Ought," 3, 9

PAIN, 150, 173
Permanence of values, 186 f.
Personal immortality, 186
Philosophy, moral, 1, 6 f., 193 f.
Pitt-Rivers, Mr. G., 131
Plato, *Gorgias*, 68
Pleasure, 173
——, Aristotle on, 73, 77, 94 f., 149
Politics, Greek, 72
Practice, moral, 5, 193 f.
Production and action, 98 f.
Psychological fallacy, 131, 139
Punishment and reward, 81, 187
Purpose, 68 f., 89, 105, 121

RASHDALL, Dr. H., 155
Reason, 46
—— and feeling, 86, 155 f.
——, Aristotle on, 79, 86
——, Kant on, 27
——, Practical, 46 f.
——, Sidgwick on, 61
Respect, Kant on, 21
Reward and punishment, 81, 187
Right, 9, 22, 179
—— as universality 25

SATISFACTION, 125
Seeley, Sir J. R., 92
Self, Kant on the pure, 34 f.
Self-sacrifice, 38, 145
Sidgwick, Prof. H., on goodness, 60 f.
—— —— ——, on reason, 61
State, Greek, 69, 72
Stephen, Sir J. F., 189 n.
Stout, Dr. G. F., 95

THEISM, 185
Theology, Catholic, 103
Titchener, Prof. E. B., 97 n.

UNIVERSALITY, 23, 25, 35 f., 40 f., 45
——, Aristotle on, 82
Utilitarianism, 58 f., 168, 173

VALUE, 49, 146 f.
——, Moral, 179
——, Permanence of, 186 f.
Voluntary action, 89

WALLAS, Mr. G., 84
Westermarck, Prof. E., 155
Will, 89
——, Freedom of the, 191
——, Kant on the, 19 f., 28, 32
——, Supreme, 186
Worth, moral, 4, 20